Kivy – Interactive Applications and Games in Python
Second Edition

Create responsive cross-platform UI/UX applications
and games in Python using the open source Kivy library

Roberto Ulloa

BIRMINGHAM - MUMBAI

Kivy – Interactive Applications and Games in Python
Second Edition

First published: September 2013

Second edition: June 2015

Production reference: 1240615

Published by Packt Publishing Ltd.
Livery Place
35 Livery Street
Birmingham B3 2PB, UK.

ISBN 978-1-78528-692-6

www.packtpub.com

Credits

Author
Roberto Ulloa

Reviewers
Takumi Adachi
Philip Bjorge
Joe Dorocak
Vijay Mahrra
Edward C. Delaporte V

Commissioning Editor
Nadeem N. Bagban

Acquisition Editor
Nikhil Karkal

Content Development Editor
Amey Varangaonkar

Technical Editor
Ankur Ghiye

Copy Editor
Adithi Shetty

Project Coordinator
Suzanne Coutinho

Proofreader
Safis Editing

Indexer
Priya Sane

Graphics
Sheetal Aute
Disha Haria
Jason Monteiro

Production Coordinator
Nitesh Thakur

Cover Work
Nitesh Thakur

About the Author

Roberto Ulloa has a diverse academic record in multiple disciplines within the field of computer science. Currently, he is working with artificial societies as part of his PhD thesis at the University of Western Ontario. He obtained an MSc degree from the University of Costa Rica and taught programming and computer networking there. He has earned a living as a web developer, working with Python/Django and PHP/Wordpress. He collaborates with various researchers while also working on his own projects, including his blog (`http://robertour.com`). He constantly worries that the Internet has already become aware of itself and that we are not able to communicate with it because of the improbability of it being able to speak any of the 6,000-plus odd human languages that exist on the planet.

I would like to thank Celina for supporting me in all my adventures, in particular, this book. I am very grateful for the valuable contributions and feedback of the Packt Publishing team, the editors, and the reviewers. Also, I would like to thank all those people who made the previous edition possible. Their ideas and encouragement made that edition a success, which is why I have now been given the opportunity to update and expand it with this second edition.

About the Reviewers

Takumi Adachi is an avid user and programmer of web and mobile applications. His strong points include HTML/CSS, JavaScript and its many frameworks and libraries, and Android development. He has also contributed a little to *Kivy Blueprints*, *Mark Vasilkov*, *Packt Publishing*.

> I want to thank my family, friends, Justin, and my past and present employers for helping me get to where I am today.

Philip Bjorge is a full-stack developer who has worked on projects for health, amusement parks, academics, and high-tech industries. Prior to joining Substantial, a Seattle-based software design agency, he worked on the Xbox Music and Video team at Microsoft. Most notably, he was a developer for Surface Music Kit, an app that was featured at the Surface 2 press conference unveiling and was on display in Microsoft stores nationwide.

Joe Dorocak, whose Internet moniker is Joe Codeswell, is a very experienced programmer. He enjoys creating readable code that implements project requirements efficiently and in a manner that can be easily understood. He considers writing code akin to writing poetry. He crafts his code so it acts as communication, not only with the machine platforms on which it runs, but also with the human programmers who will read it in the future.

Joe has been employed directly and also in a contractual role by start-ups and by many major top-shelf companies, including IBM, HP, and GTE/Sprint.

Joe is presently concentrating on application and web project consulting using languages, frameworks, and tools and techniques, including Python, JavaScript, web2py, Cython, memoization, and other performance enhancement techniques. For more details on him, please visit `https://www.linkedin.com/in/joedorocak`.

Joe has also worked on *Kivy Blueprints* by Mark Vasilko and *Functional Programming in JavaScript* by Dan Mantyla.

I am very grateful to Suzanne Coutinho and Nidhi Joshi of Packt Publishing. They have always coordinated my efforts wisely, professionally, and with a consistent human touch.

Vijay Mahrra is an experienced system administrator, developer, and programmer with over 20 years of experience from the very early days of the Web to the present day, contributing his knowledge and experience to various free and open source projects along the way.

You can find out more about him at `http://about.me/vijay.mahrra`

A big thank you to my mother, Nirmal; niece, Shreya; and everyone at Packt Publishing. Thanks to Matt Saunders and Neil Levine for all the years of hosting.

Edward C. Delaporte V has been creating and using software since the mid 1980s.

Edward wants to thank all of the software developers who wrote the code he learned from, especially those who took the time to also write about their code, how to program, and how to program well.

www.PacktPub.com

Support files, eBooks, discount offers, and more

For support files and downloads related to your book, please visit www.PacktPub.com.

Did you know that Packt offers eBook versions of every book published, with PDF and ePub files available? You can upgrade to the eBook version at www.PacktPub.com and as a print book customer, you are entitled to a discount on the eBook copy. Get in touch with us at service@packtpub.com for more details.

At www.PacktPub.com, you can also read a collection of free technical articles, sign up for a range of free newsletters and receive exclusive discounts and offers on Packt books and eBooks.

https://www2.packtpub.com/books/subscription/packtlib

Do you need instant solutions to your IT questions? PacktLib is Packt's online digital book library. Here, you can search, access, and read Packt's entire library of books.

Why subscribe?

- Fully searchable across every book published by Packt
- Copy and paste, print, and bookmark content
- On demand and accessible via a web browser

Free access for Packt account holders

If you have an account with Packt at www.PacktPub.com, you can use this to access PacktLib today and view 9 entirely free books. Simply use your login credentials for immediate access.

Table of Contents

Preface

Mobile devices have transformed the way applications are perceived. They have increased in interaction types; the user now expects gestures, multi-touches, animations, responsiveness, virtual keyboards, and magic-pens. Moreover, compatibility has become a must if you want to avoid the barriers imposed by major operating systems. Kivy is an open source Python solution that covers these market needs with an easy-to-learn and rapid development approach. Kivy continues to grow fast and two versions have been released since the first publication of this book in September 2013. Thanks to an enthusiastic community, Kivy is making its way in an extremely competitive territory in which it stands out for offering both a cross-platform and efficient alternative to native development and HTML5.

This book introduces you to the Kivy world, covering a large variety of important topics related to interactive applications and games development. The components presented in this book were selected according to their usefulness for developing state-of-art applications and also for serving as an example of broader Kivy functionalities. Following this approach, the book covers a big part of the Kivy library.

This book provides you with examples to understand their use and how to integrate the three projects that come with this book. The first one, the comic creator, exemplifies how to build a user interface (*Chapter 1, GUI Basics – Building an Interface*), how to draw vector shapes in the screen (*Chapter 2, Graphics – the Canvas*), how to bind user interactions with pieces codes (*Chapter 3, Widget Events – Binding Actions*), and other components related to improving the user experience (*Chapter 4, Improving the User Experience*). The second project, Invaders Revenge, is an interactive game that introduces you to the use of animations, scheduling of tasks, keyboard events, and multi-touch control (*Chapter 5, Invaders Revenge – an Interactive Multi-touch Game*). The third project, Kivy Player, teaches how we can control video streams with a modern design and responsive interactions to maximize the use of the screen (*Chapter 6, Kivy Player – a TED Video Streamer*).

Occasionally, this book explains some technical but important Kivy concepts that are related to the Kivy class structure and implementation, or the order and strategies to draw on the screen. These explanations give the reader some insights into the Kivy internals that will help them solve potential problems when they develop their own projects. Even though they are not necessary for the comprehension of the main topics of this book, they will become important lessons when the reader faces new situations implementing their own applications.

This book grabs the reader's attention by stating interesting programming scenarios. The sections are generally short and straightforward, making the learning process constant. These short sections will also serve as a reference when the reader finishes the book. However, serving as a reference doesn't prevent the text from achieving the main goal, which is teaching bigger projects that connect the small topics. At the end of this book, the reader will feel comfortable to start their own project.

What this book covers

Chapter 1, GUI Basics – Building an Interface, introduces the basic components and layouts of Kivy and how to integrate them through the Kivy Language.

Chapter 2, Graphics – the Canvas, explains the use of the canvas and how to draw vector figures on the screen.

Chapter 3, Widget Events – Binding Actions, teaches how to connect the interactions of the user through the interface with particular code inside the program.

Chapter 4, Improving the User Experience, introduces a collection of useful components to enrich the interaction of the user with the interface.

Chapter 5, Invaders Revenge – an Interactive Multi-touch Game, presents components and strategies to build highly interactive applications.

Chapter 6, Kivy Player – a TED Video Streamer, builds a responsive and professional-looking interface to control a video stream service.

What you need for this book

You need to have some programming experience before starting this book and specifically have a good understanding of some software engineering concepts, particularly inheritance and the difference between classes and instances. You should be already familiar with Python. That said, the code is kept as simple as possible and it avoids the use of very specific Python nuances, so any other developer can follow it. No previous experience of Kivy is required, though some general programming knowledge of event handling, scheduling, and user interfaces would boost your learning. You also need to have Kivy 1.9.0 installed with all its requirements. The installation instructions can be found at `http://kivy.org/docs/gettingstarted/installation.html`.

Who this book is for

The book aims at developers, specifically Python developers, who want to create UI/UX applications for different platforms. This book will also benefit developers that are seeking for an alternative to HTML5 or native Android/iOS development, looking forward to learn about mobile development and its demands (multi-touch, gestures, and animations), or wishing to improve their understanding of object-oriented topics such as inheritance, classes and instances, and event handling.

Conventions

In this book, you will find a number of text styles that distinguish between different kinds of information. Here are some examples of these styles and an explanation of their meaning.

Code words in text, database table names, folder names, filenames, file extensions, pathnames, dummy URLs, user input, and Twitter handles are shown as follows: "This is the reason we included the `on_touch_down` event."

A block of code is set as follows:

```
1.  # File name: hello.py
2.  import kivy
3.  kivy.require('1.9.0')
4.
5.  from kivy.app import App
6.  from kivy.uix.button import Label
7.
8.  class HelloApp(App):
9.      def build(self):
10.         return Label(text='Hello World!')
11.
12. if __name__=="__main__":
13.         HelloApp().run()
```

The numeration restarts at the beginning of each chapter providing a unique identifier to each line code. Code from previous chapter will never be referenced, instead it will be copied again if needed. When we wish to draw your attention to a particular part of a code block, the relevant lines or items are set in bold, for example, line 10.

New terms and **important words** are shown in bold. Words that you see on the screen, for example, in menus or dialog boxes, appear in the text like this: "We need an alternate way to stop the video (different from the **Stop** button)."

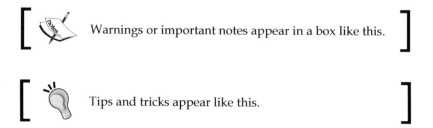

Warnings or important notes appear in a box like this.

Tips and tricks appear like this.

Reader feedback

Feedback from our readers is always welcome. Let us know what you think about this book—what you liked or disliked. Reader feedback is important for us as it helps us develop titles that you will really get the most out of.

To send us general feedback, simply e-mail feedback@packtpub.com, and mention the book's title in the subject of your message.

If there is a topic that you have expertise in and you are interested in either writing or contributing to a book, see our author guide at www.packtpub.com/authors.

Customer support

Now that you are the proud owner of a Packt book, we have a number of things to help you to get the most from your purchase.

Downloading the example code

You can download the example code files from your account at http://www.packtpub.com for all the Packt Publishing books you have purchased. If you purchased this book elsewhere, you can visit http://www.packtpub.com/support and register to have the files e-mailed directly to you.

Errata

Although we have taken every care to ensure the accuracy of our content, mistakes do happen. If you find a mistake in one of our books—maybe a mistake in the text or the code—we would be grateful if you could report this to us. By doing so, you can save other readers from frustration and help us improve subsequent versions of this book. If you find any errata, please report them by visiting http://www.packtpub.com/submit-errata, selecting your book, clicking on the **Errata Submission Form** link, and entering the details of your errata. Once your errata are verified, your submission will be accepted and the errata will be uploaded to our website or added to any list of existing errata under the Errata section of that title.

To view the previously submitted errata, go to https://www.packtpub.com/books/content/support and enter the name of the book in the search field. The required information will appear under the **Errata** section.

Piracy

Piracy of copyrighted material on the Internet is an ongoing problem across all media. At Packt, we take the protection of our copyright and licenses very seriously. If you come across any illegal copies of our works in any form on the Internet, please provide us with the location address or website name immediately so that we can pursue a remedy.

Please contact us at copyright@packtpub.com with a link to the suspected pirated material.

We appreciate your help in protecting our authors and our ability to bring you valuable content.

Questions

If you have a problem with any aspect of this book, you can contact us at questions@packtpub.com, and we will do our best to address the problem.

1
GUI Basics – Building an Interface

Kivy is a free, open source Python library that allows for quick and easy development of highly interactive multiplatform applications. Kivy's execution speed is comparable to the native mobile alternative, Java for Android or Objective C for iOS. Moreover, Kivy has the huge advantage of being able to run on multiple platforms, just as HTML5 does; in which case, Kivy performs better because it doesn't rely on a heavy browser, and many of its components are implemented in C using the Cython library in such a way that most of the graphics processing runs directly in the GPU. Kivy strikes a great balance between performance and portability across various hardware and software environments. Kivy emerges with a simple but ambitious goal in mind:

> *"... same code for every platform, at least what we use every day: Linux/Windows/ Mac OS X/Android/iOS"*

Mathieu Virbel (`http://txzone.net/2011/01/kivy-next-pymt-on-android-step-1-done/`)

This support has being extended to Raspberry Pi, thanks to a crowd funding campaign started by Mathieu Virbel, the creator of Kivy. Kivy was introduced for the first time at EuroPython 2011 as a Python framework designed for creating natural user interfaces. Since then, it has grown bigger and attracted an enthusiastic community.

This book requires some knowledge of Python, and very basic terminal skills, but also it requires some understanding of **Object-Oriented Programming (OOP)** concepts. In particular, it is assumed that you understand the concept of **inheritance** and the difference between **instances** and **classes**. Refer to the following table to review some of these concepts:

Concept	URL
OOP	`http://en.wikipedia.org/wiki/Object-oriented_ programming`
Inheritance	`http://en.wikipedia.org/wiki/Inheritance_(object- oriented_programming)`
Instance	`http://en.wikipedia.org/wiki/Instance_(computer_ science)`
Class	`http://en.wikipedia.org/wiki/Class_(computer_ science)`

Before we start, you will need to install Kivy. The installation process for all different platforms is documented and regularly updated on the Kivy website: `http://kivy. org/docs/installation/installation.html`.

All code in this book has been tested with Kivy 1.9.0 and both Python 2.7 and Python 3.4 (but 3.3 should work fine as well).

Note that packaging support for mobile is not yet complete for Python 3.3+. For now, if we want to create mobile apps for Android or iOS, we should use Python 2.7. If you want to know your Python version, you can execute `python -V` in a terminal to check your installed Python version.

In this chapter, we start by creating user interfaces using one of Kivy's most fun and powerful components – the Kivy language (`.kv`). The Kivy Language separates logic from presentation in order to keep an easy and intuitive code; it also links components at an interface level. In future chapters, you will also learn how to build and modify interfaces dynamically using pure Python code and Kivy as a library.

Here is a list of all the skills that you are about to learn:

- Launching a Kivy application
- Using the Kivy language
- Instantiating and personalizing widgets (GUI components) through basic properties and variables
- Differentiating between fixed, proportional, absolute, and relative coordinates
- Creating responsive GUIs through layouts
- Modularizing code in different files

This chapter covers all the basics for building a **Graphical User Interface (GUI)** in Kivy. First, we will learn techniques to run an application and how to use and integrate widgets. After that, we will introduce the main project of the book, the *Comic Creator*, and program the main structure of the GUI that we will continue using in the following two chapters. At the end of this chapter, you will be able to build a GUI starting from a pencil and paper sketch, and also learn some techniques to make the GUI responsive to the size of the window.

Basic interface – Hello World!

Let's put our hands on our first code.

Downloading the example code

You can download the example code files for all Packt books you have purchased from your account at http://www.packtpub.com. If you purchased this book elsewhere, you can visit http://www.packtpub.com/support and register to have the files e-mailed directly to you.

The following is a Hello World program:

```
1.  # File name: hello.py
2.  import kivy
3.  kivy.require('1.9.0')
4.
5.  from kivy.app import App
6.  from kivy.uix.button import Label
7.
8.  class HelloApp(App):
9.      def build(self):
10.             return Label(text='Hello World!')
11.
12. if __name__=="__main__":
13.             HelloApp().run()
```

 This is merely Python code. Launching a Kivy program is not any different from launching any other Python application.

In order to run the code, you open a terminal (line of commands or console) and specify the following command in Windows or Linux: `python hello.py --size=150x100` (`--size` is a parameter to specify the screen size).

On a Mac, you must type in `kivy` instead of `python` after installing `Kivy.app` in `/Applications`. Lines 2 and 3 verify that we have the appropriate version of Kivy installed on our computer.

 If you try to launch our application with an older Kivy version (say 1.8.0) than the specified version, then line 3 will raise an `Exception` error. This `Exception` is not raised if we have a more recent version.

We omit the call to `kivy.require` in most of the examples in the book, but you will find it in the code that you download online (`https://www.packtpub.com/`), and its use is strongly encouraged in real-life projects. The program uses two classes from the Kivy library (lines 5 and 6) – `App` and `Label`. The class **App** is the starting point of any Kivy application. Consider `App` as the empty window where we will add other Kivy components.

We use the App class through **inheritance**; the App class becomes the base class of the HelloApp subclass or child class (line 8). In practice, this means that the HelloApp class has all the variables and methods of App, plus whatever we define in the body (lines 9 and 10) of the HelloApp class. Most importantly, App is the starting point of any Kivy application. We can see that line 13 creates an instance of HelloApp and runs it.

Now the HelloApp class's body just overrides one of the existing App class's methods, the build(self) method. This method has to return the window content. In our case, a **Label** that holds the text **Hello World**! (line 10). A **Label** is a **widget** that allows you to display some text on the screen.

 A **widget** is a Kivy GUI component. Widgets are the minimal graphical units that we put together in order to create user interfaces.

The following screenshot shows the resulting screen after executing the hello.py code:

So, is Kivy just another library for Python? Well, yes. But as part of the library, Kivy offers its own language in order to separate the logic from the presentation and to link elements of the interface. Moreover, remember that this library will allow you to port your applications to many platforms.

Let's start to explore the Kivy language. We will separate the previous Python code into two files, one for the presentation (interface), and another for the logic. The first file includes the Python lines:

```
14. # File name: hello2.py
15. from kivy.app import App
16. from kivy.uix.button import Label
17.
18. class Hello2App(App):
```

```
19.     def build(self):
20.         return Label()
21.
22. if __name__=="__main__":
23.     Hello2App().run()
```

The `hello2.py` code is very similar to `hello.py`. The difference is that the method `build(self)` doesn't have the **Hello World!** message. Instead, the message has been moved to the `text` property in the Kivy language file (`hello2.kv`).

 A **property** is an attribute that can be used to change the content, appearance, or behavior of a widget.

The following is the code (rules) of `hello2.kv`, which shows how we modify the `Label` content with the `text` property (line 27):

```
24. # File name: hello2.kv
25. #:kivy 1.9.0
26. <Label>:
27.     text: 'Hello World!'
```

You might wonder how Python or Kivy knows that these two files (`hello2.py` and `hello2.kv`) are related. This tends to be confusing at the beginning. The key is in the name of the subclass of `App`, which in this case is `HelloApp`.

 The beginning part of the `App` class's subclass name must coincide with the name of the Kivy file. For example, if the definition of the class is `class FooApp(App)`, then the name of the file has to be `foo.kv` and in the same directory of the main file (the one that executes the `run()` method of `App`).

Once that consideration is included, this example can be run in the same way we ran the previous one. We just need to be sure we are calling the main file – `python hello2.py --size=150x100`.

This is our first contact with the Kivy language, so we should have an in-depth look at it. Line 25 (`hello2.kv`) tells Python the minimal version of Kivy that should be used. It does the same thing as the previous lines 2 and 3 do in `hello.py`. The instructions that start with `#:` in the header of a Kivy language are called **directives**. We will also be omitting the version directive throughout the rest of this book, but remember to include it in your own projects.

The `<Label>:` rule (line 26) indicates that we are going to modify the `Label` class.

 The Kivy language is expressed as a sequence of rules. A **rule** is a piece of code that defines the content, behavior, and appearance of a Kivy widget class. A rule always starts with a widget class name in angle brackets followed by a colon, like this, `<Widget Class>:`

Inside the rule, we set the `text` property with `'Hello World!'` (line 27). The code in this section will generate the same output screen as before. In general, everything in Kivy can be done using pure Python and importing the necessary classes from the Kivy library, as we did in the first example (`hello.py`). However, there are many advantages of using the Kivy language and therefore this book explains all the presentation programming in the Kivy language, unless we need to add dynamic components, in which case using Kivy as a traditional Python library is more appropriate.

If you are an experienced programmer, you might have worried that modifying the `Label` class affects all the instances we could potentially create from `Label`, and therefore they will all contain the same `Hello World` text. That is true, and we are going to study a better approach to doing this in the following section.

Basic widgets – labels and buttons

In the last section, we used the `Label` class, which is one of the multiple widgets that Kivy provides. You can think of widgets as interface blocks that we use to set up a GUI. Kivy has a complete set of widgets – buttons, labels, checkboxes, dropdowns, and many more. You can find them all in the API of Kivy under the package `kivy.uix` (`http://kivy.org/docs/api-kivy.html`).

We are going to learn the basics of how to create our own personalized widget without affecting the default configuration of Kivy widgets. In order to do that, we will use inheritance to create the `MyWidget` class in the `widgets.py` file:

```
28.# File name: widgets.py
29. from kivy.app import App
30. from kivy.uix.widget import Widget
31.
32. class MyWidget(Widget):
33.     pass
34.
35. class WidgetsApp(App):
```

```
36.     def build(self):
37.         return MyWidget()
38.
39. if __name__=="__main__":
40.     WidgetsApp().run()
```

In line 32, we inherit from the base class **Widget** and create the subclass MyWidget. It is a general practice to create your own Widget for your applications instead of using the Kivy classes directly, because we want to avoid applying our changes to all future instances of the widget Kivy class. In the case of our previous example (hello2.kv), modifying the Label class (line 26) would affect all of its future instances. In line 37, we instantiated MyWidget instead of Label directly (as we did in hello2.py), so we can now distinguish between our widget (MyWidget) and the Kivy widget (Widget). The rest of the code is analogous to what we covered before.

The following is the corresponding Kivy language code (widgets.kv):

```
41. # File name: widgets.kv
42. <MyWidget>:
43.     Button:
44.         text: 'Hello'
45.         font_size: 32
46.         color: .8,.9,0,1
47.         pos: 0, 100
48.         size: 100, 50
49.     Button:
50.         text: 'World!'
51.         font_size: 32
52.         color: .8,.9,0,1
53.         pos: 100,0
54.         size: 100, 50
```

Note that now we are using **buttons** instead of labels. Most of the basic widgets in Kivy work in similar ways. In fact, **Button** is just a subclass of Label that incorporates more properties such as background color.

Compare the notation of line 26 (<Label>:) in hello2.kv with line 43 (Button:) of the preceding code (widgets.kv). We used the rule class notation (<Class>:) for the Label (and MyWidget) class, but a different notation (Instance:) for Button. In this way, we defined that MyWidget has two instances of Button (line 43 and 49).

Finally, we set the properties of the `Button` instances. The **font_size** property sets the size of the text. The **color** property sets the text color and is specified in RGBA format (red, green, blue, and alpha/transparency). The properties **size** and **pos** set the size and position of the widget and consist of a pair of **fixed coordinates** (x for horizontal and y for vertical), the exact pixels on the window.

 Note that the coordinate (0, 0) is located at the bottom-left corner, the Cartesian origin. Many other languages (including CSS) use the top-left corner as the (0, 0) coordinate, so take note!

The following screenshot shows the output of `widgets.py` and `widgets.kv` with some helpful annotations:

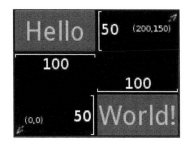

A couple of things can be improved in the previous code (`widgets.kv`). First, there are some repeated properties for both buttons: `pos`, `color`, and `font_size`. Instead of that, let's create our own `Button` as we did with `MyWidget` so it will be easy to keep the buttons' design consistent. Second, the fixed position is quite annoying because the widgets don't adjust when the screen is resized. Let's make it responsive to the screen size in the `widgets2.kv` file:

```
55. # File name: widgets2.kv
56. <MyButton@Button>:
57.     color: .8,.9,0,1
58.     font_size: 32
59.     size: 100, 50
60.
61. <MyWidget>:
62.     MyButton:
63.         text: 'Hello'
64.         pos: root.x, root.top - self.height
65.     MyButton:
66.         text: 'World!'
67.         pos: root.right - self.width, root.y
```

In this code (`widgets2.kv`), we create (`<MyButton@Button>:`) and customize the `MyButton` class (lines 56 to 59) and instances (line 62 to 67). Note the differences in the manner we defined `MyWidget` and `MyButton`.

> Because we did not define the `MyButton` base class in `widgets.py` as we did with `MyWidget` (line 32 of `widgets.py`), we have to specify `@Class` in the Kivy language rule (line 56). In the `MyWidget` class case, we also needed to define its class from the Python side because we instantiated it directly (line 37 of `widgets.py`).

In this example, each `Button` class's position is responsive in the sense that they are always in the corners of the screen, no matter what the window size is. In order to achieve that, we need to use two internal variables – **self** and **root**. You might be familiar with the variable **self**. As you have probably guessed, it is just a reference to the `Widget` itself. For example, `self.height` (line 64) has a value of `50` because that is the height of that particular `MyButton` class. The variable **root** is a reference to the `Widget` class at the top of the hierarchy. For example, the `root.x` (line 64) has a value of `0` because that is the position in X-axis of the `MyWidget` instance created on line 37 of `widgets.py`.

`MyWidget` uses all of the window's space by default; therefore, the origin is (0, 0). The **x** and **y** and **width** and **height** are also widget properties, which we can use to disjoint `pos` and `size` respectively.

Fixed coordinates are still a laborious way to organize widgets and elements in the window. Let's move on to something smarter – layouts.

Layouts

No doubt, fixed coordinates are the most flexible way to organize elements in an n-dimensional space; however, it is very time consuming. Instead, Kivy provides a set of layouts that will facilitate the work of organizing widgets. A **Layout** is a `Widget` subclass that implements different strategies to organize embedded widgets. For example, one strategy could be organizing widgets in a grid (`GridLayout`).

Let's start with a simple **FloatLayout** example. It works in a very similar manner to the way we organize widgets directly inside of another `Widget` subclass, except that now we can use **proportional coordinates** ("percentages" of the total size of the window) rather than fixed coordinates (exact pixels).

That means that we won't need the calculations we did in the previous section with
`self` and `root`. Here is the Python code of an example that resembles the previous
one:

```
68. # File name: floatlayout.py
69.
70. from kivy.app import App
71. from kivy.uix.floatlayout import FloatLayout
72.
73. class FloatLayoutApp(App):
74.     def build(self):
75.         return FloatLayout()
76.
77. if __name__=="__main__":
78.     FloatLayoutApp().run()
```

There is nothing really new in the preceding code (`floatlayout.py`), except the
use of `FloatLayout` (line 75). The interesting parts are in the corresponding Kivy
language (`floatlayout.kv`):

```
79. # File name: floatlayout.py
80. <Button>:
81.     color: .8,.9,0,1
82.     font_size: 32
83.     size_hint: .4, .3
84.
85. <FloatLayout>:
86.     Button:
87.         text: 'Hello'
88.         pos_hint: {'x': 0, 'top': 1}
89.     Button:
90.         text: 'World!'
91.         pos_hint: {'right': 1, 'y': 0}
```

In `floatlayout.kv`, we use two new properties – **size_hint** (line 83) and **pos_
hint** (lines 88 and 91) .They are similar to `size` and `pos` but receive proportional
coordinates with values ranging from 0 to 1; (0, 0) is the bottom-left corner and (1,
1) is the top-right corner. For example, the `size_hint` property on line 83 sets the
width to 40 percent of the window width and the height to 30 percent of the current
window height. Something similar happens to the `pos_hint` property (lines 88 and
91 but the notation is different – a Python dictionary where the keys (for example,
`'x'` or `'top'`) indicate which part of the widget is referenced. For example, `'x'`
is the left border.

Note that we use the `top` key instead of the `y` one on line 88 and the `right` key instead of the `x` one on line 91. The **top** and **right** keys respectively reference the top and right edges of `Button`. In this case, we could have also used `x` and `y` for both axes; for example, we could have written `pos_hint: {'x': .85, 'y': 0}` as line 91. However, the **right** and **top** keys avoid us some calculations, making the code clearer.

The next screenshot shows the result, and the available keys for the `pos_hint` dictionary:

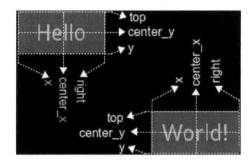

The available `pos_hint` keys (`x`, **center_x**, `right`, `y`, **center_y**, and `top`) are useful to align the edges or for centering. For example, `pos_hint: {'center_x':.5, 'center_y':.5}` would align a widget in the middle no matter the size of the window.

We could have used the `top` and `right` properties with the fixed positioning of `widgets2.kv` (line 64 and 67), but note that `pos` doesn't accept Python dictionaries (`{'x':0,'y':0}`), just pairs of values exclusively corresponding to (x, y). Therefore, instead of using the `pos` property, we should use the `x`, `center_x`, `right`, `y`, `center_y`, and `top` properties directly (not dictionary keys). For example, instead of `pos: root.x, root.top - self.height` (line 64), we should have used:

```
x: 0
top: root.height
```

The properties `x`, `center_x`, `right`, `y`, `center_y`, and `top` always specify **fixed coordinates** (pixels), and not proportional ones. If we want to use **proportional coordinates**, we have to be inside a `Layout` (or an `App`) and use the `pos_hint` property.

We can also force a Layout to use fixed values, but there can be conflicts if we are not careful with the properties. If we use any Layout; pos_hint and size_hint take priority. If we want to use fixed positioning properties (pos, x, center_x, right, y, center_y, top), we have to ensure that we are not using the pos_hint property. Second, if we want to use the size, height, or width properties, then we need to set a None value to the size_hint axis we want to use with absolute values. For example, size_hint: (None, .10) allows us to use height property, but it keeps the width of 10 percent for the window's size.

The following table summarizes what we have seen about the positioning and sizing properties. The first and second columns indicate the name of the property and its respective value. The third and fourth column indicate whether it is available for layouts and for widgets.

Property	Value	For layouts	For widgets
size_hint	A pair w, h: w, and h express a proportion (from 0 to 1 or None).	Yes	No
size_ hint_x size_ hint_y	A proportion from 0 to 1 or None, indicating width (size_ hint_x) or height (size_ hint_y).	Yes	No
pos_hint	Dictionary with one x-axis key (x, center_x, or right) and one y-axis key (y, center_y, or top). The values are proportions from 0 to 1.	Yes	No
size	A pair w, h: w and h indicating fixed width and height in pixels.	Yes, but set size_ hint: (None, None)	Yes
width	Fixed number of pixels.	Yes, but set size_ hint_x: None	Yes
height	Fixed number of pixels.	Yes, but set size_ hint_y: None	Yes

Property	Value	For layouts	For widgets
`pos`	A pair x, y indicating a fixed coordinate (x, y) in pixels.	Yes, but don't use `pos_hint`	Yes
`x, right or center_x`	Fixed number of pixels.	Yes, but don't use `x`, `right` or `center_x` in `pos_hint`	Yes
`y, top or center_y`	Fixed number of pixels.	Yes, but don't use `y`, `top` or `center_y` in `pos_hint`	Yes

We have to be careful because some of the properties behave differently depending on the layout we are using. Kivy currently has eight different layouts, which are described in the following table. The left-hand side column shows the name of the Kivy layout class. The right-hand side column describes briefly how they work.

Layout	Details
`FloatLayout`	Organizes the widgets with proportional coordinates by the `size_hint` and `pos_hint` properties. The values are numbers between 0 and 1, indicating a proportion to the window size.
`RelativeLayout`	Operates in the same way that `FloatLayout` does, but the positioning properties (pos, x, center_x, right, y, center_y, top) are relative to the Layout size and not the window size.
`GridLayout`	Organizes widgets in a grid. You have to specify at least one of two properties – `cols` (for columns) or `rows` (for rows).
`BoxLayout`	Organizes widgets in one row or one column depending on whether the value of the `orientation` property is `horizontal` or `vertical`.
`StackLayout`	Similar to `BoxLayout`, but it goes to the next row or column when it runs out of space. There is more flexibility to set the `orientation`. For example, `rl-bt` organizes the widgets in right-to-left, bottom-to-top order. Any combination of `lr` (left to right), `rl` (right to left), `tb` (top to bottom), and `bt` (bottom to top) is allowed.

Layout	Details
`ScatterLayout`	Works in a similar manner to `RelativeLayout` but allows multitouch gesturing for rotating, scaling, and translating. It is slightly different in its implementation, so we will review it later on.
`PageLayout`	Stacks widgets on top of each other, creating a multipage effect that allows flipping of pages using side borders. Very often, we will use another layout to organize elements inside each of the pages, which are simply widgets.

The Kivy API (`http://kivy.org/docs/api-kivy.html`) offers a detailed explanation and good examples of each of the layouts. The behavioral difference of the properties depends on the layout, and it is sometimes unexpected. Here are some hints that will help us in the GUI building process:

- `size_hint`, `size_hint_x`, and `size_hint_y` work on all the layouts (except `PageLayout`), but the behavior might be different. For example, `GridLayout` will try to take an average of the x hints and y hints on the same row or column respectively.

- You should use values from 0 to 1 with `size_hint`, `size_hint_x`, and `size_hint_y`. However, you can use values higher than 1. Depending on the layout, Kivy makes the widget bigger than the container or tries to recalculate a proportion based on the sum of the hints on the same axis.

- `pos_hint` only works for `FloatLayout`, `RelativeLayout`, and `BoxLayout`. In `BoxLayout`, only the axis-x keys (`x`, `center_x`, `right`) work in the `vertical` orientation and vice-versa for the `horizontal` orientation. An analogous rule applies for the fixed positioning properties (`pos`, `x`, `center_x`, `right`, `y`, `center_y`, and `top`).

- `size_hint`, `size_hint_x`, and `size_hint_y` can always be set as `None` in favor of `size`, `width`, and `height`.

There are more properties and particularities of each layout, but with the ones covered, we will be able to build almost any GUI. In general, the recommendation is to use the layout as it is and, instead of forcing it with the properties we are using, it is better to have more layouts and combine them to reach our goals. The next section will teach us how to embed layouts and will offer more comprehensive examples.

Embedding layouts

Layouts are subclasses of widgets. We have already been embedding widgets inside widgets since the beginning (line 43) and it won't matter if the widgets we are embedding are also layouts. In this section, we will work with a comprehensive example to explore the effect of the position properties discussed in the previous section. The example is not visually appealing, but it will be useful to illustrate some concepts and to provide some code that you can use to test different properties. The following is the Python code (`layouts.py`) for the example:

```
92.  # File name: layouts.py
93.  from kivy.app import App
94.  from kivy.uix.gridlayout import GridLayout
95.
96.  class MyGridLayout(GridLayout):
97.      pass
98.
99.  class LayoutsApp(App):
100. def build(self):
101.     return MyGridLayout()
102.
103. if __name__=="__main__":
104.     LayoutsApp().run()
```

Nothing new in the preceding code – we just created `MyGridLayout`. The final output is shown in the next screenshot, with some indications about the different layouts:

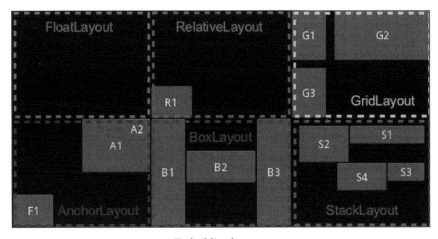

Embedding layouts

In this screenshot, six different Kivy layouts are embedded into a **GridLayout** of two rows (line 107) in order to show the behavior of different widget properties. The code is straightforward, although extensive. Therefore, we are going to study the corresponding Kivy language code (`layouts.kv`) in five fragments. The following is fragment 1:

```
105. # File name: layouts.kv (Fragment 1)
106. <MyGridLayout>:
107.     rows: 2
108.     FloatLayout:
109.         Button:
110.             text: 'F1'
111.             size_hint: .3, .3
112.             pos: 0, 0
113.     RelativeLayout:
114.         Button:
115.             text: 'R1'
116.             size_hint: .3, .3
117.             pos: 0, 0
```

In this code, `MyGridLayout` is defined by the number of rows with the **rows** property (line 107). Then we add the first two layouts – `FloatLayout` and **RelativeLayout** with one `Button` each. Both buttons have a defined property of `pos: 0, 0` (lines 112 and 117) but note in the previous screenshot that the `Button` **F1** (line 109) is in the bottom-left corner of the whole window, whereas the `Button` **R1** (line 114) is in the bottom-left corner of `RelativeLayout`. The reason is that the `pos` coordinates in `FloatLayout` are not relative to the position of the layout.

> Note that `pos_hint` always uses relative coordinates, no matter the layout we are using. In other words, the previous example wouldn't have worked if we were using `pos_hint` instead of `pos`.

In fragment 2, one **GridLayout** is added to `MyGridLayout`:

```
118. # File name: layouts.kv (Fragment 2)
119. GridLayout:
120.     cols: 2
121.     spacing: 10
122.     Button:
123.         text: 'G1'
```

```
124.            size_hint_x: None
125.            width: 50
126.      Button:
127.            text: 'G2'
126.      Button:
128.            text: 'G3'
129.            size_hint_x: None
130.            width: 50
```

In this case, we use the **cols** property to define two columns (line 120) and the spacing property to separate the internal widgets by 10 pixels from each other (line 121). Also, note in the previous screenshot that the first column is thinner than the second. We achieved this by setting the size_hint_x to None and width to 50 of the buttons **G1** (line 122) and **G3** (line 128).

In fragment 3, an **AnchorLayout** is added:

```
131. # File name: layouts.kv (Fragment 3)
132. AnchorLayout:
133.      anchor_x: 'right'
135.      anchor_y: 'top'
136.      Button:
137.            text: 'A1'
138.            size_hint: .5, .5
139.      Button:
140.            text: 'A2'
141.            size_hint: .2, .2
```

We have specified the **anchor_x** property to right and the **anchor_y** property to top (line 134 and 135) in order to arrange elements in the top-right corner of the window as shown in the previous screenshot with both buttons (lines 136 and 139). This layout is very useful to embed other layouts inside it, for example, top menu bars or side bars.

In fragment 4, a **BoxLayout** is added:

```
142. # File name: layouts.kv (Fragment 4)
143. BoxLayout:
144.      orientation: 'horizontal'
145.      Button:
146.            text: 'B1'
147.      Button:
```

```
148.          text: 'B2'
149.          size_hint: 2, .3
150.          pos_hint: {'y': .4}
151.      Button:
152.          text: 'B3'
```

The preceding code illustrates the use of BoxLayout with the **orientation** property set to horizontal. Also, the lines 149 and 150 show how to use size_hint and pos_hint to move the button **B2** further up.

Finally, fragment 5 adds a **StackLayout**:

```
153. # File name: layouts.kv (Fragment 5)
154. StackLayout:
155.     orientation: 'rl-tb'
156.     padding: 10
157.     Button:
158.         text: 'S1'
159.         size_hint: .6, .2
160.     Button:
161.         text: 'S2'
162.         size_hint: .4, .4
163.     Button:
164.         text: 'S3'
165.         size_hint: .3, .2
166.     Button:
167.         text: 'S4'
168.         size_hint: .4, .3
```

In this case, we added four buttons of different sizes. It is important to pay attention to the previous screenshot on embedding layouts to understand the rules that we applied to organize the widgets with the **orientation** property set to rl-tb (right to left, top to bottom, line 155). Also note that the **padding** property (line 156) adds 10 pixels of space between the widgets and the border of StackLayout.

PageLayout – swiping pages

The **PageLayout** works in a different manner from other layouts. It is a dynamic layout, in the sense that it allows flipping through pages using its borders. The idea is that its components are stacked in front of each other, and we can just see the one that is on top.

The following example illustrates its use, taking advantage of the example from the previous section. The Python code (`pagelayout.py`) is presented here:

```
169. # File name: pagelayout.py
170. import kivy
171.
172. from kivy.app import App
173. from kivy.uix.pagelayout import PageLayout
174.
175. class MyPageLayout(PageLayout):
176.     pass
177.
178. class PageLayoutApp(App):
179.     def build(self):
180.         return MyPageLayout()
181.
182. if __name__=="__main__":
183.     PageLayoutApp().run()
```

There is nothing new in this code except the use of the `PageLayout` class. For the Kivy language code (`pagelayout.kv`), we will study the properties of `PageLayout`. We have simply modified the `layouts.kv` studied in the previous section by changing the header of the file (lines 105 to 107), now called `pagelayout.kv`:

```
184. # File name: pagelayout.kv
185. <Layout>:
186.     canvas:
187.         Color:
188.             rgba: 1, 1, 1, 1
189.         Rectangle:
190.             pos: self.pos
191.             size: self.size
192.
193. <MyPageLayout>:
194.     page: 3
195.     border: 120
196.     swipe_threshold: .4
197.     FloatLay...
```

All the layouts inherit from a base class called `Layout`. In line 185, we are modifying this base class in the same way we did earlier with the `Button` class (line 80).

If we want to apply changes to all the child widgets that have a common base class (such as `Layout`), we can introduce those changes in the base class. Kivy will apply the changes to all the classes that derive from it.

By default, layouts don't have a background color, which is not convenient when `PageLayout` stacks them on top of each other, because we can see the elements of the layouts on the bottom. Lines 186 to 191 will draw a white (line 187 and 188) rectangle of the size (line 190) and position (line 191) of the `Layout`. In order to do this, we need to use the **canvas**, which allows us to draw shapes directly on the screen. This topic will be explained in-depth in the next chapter (*Chapter 2, Graphics - The Canvas*). You can see the result in the following screenshot:

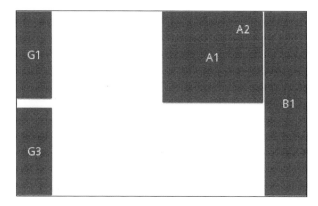

If you run the code on your computer, you will notice that it will take you to the page corresponding to `AnchorLayout` in the example of the previous section. The reason is that we set the **page** property to value 3 (line 194). Counting from 0, this property tells Kivy which page to display first. The **border** property tells Kivy how wide the side borders are (for sliding to the previous or the next screen). Finally, **swipe_threshold** tells the percentage of the screen that we have to slide over, in order to change the page. The next section will use some of the layouts and properties learned so far to display a more professional screen.

Our project – Comic Creator

We now have all the necessary concepts to be able to create any interface we want. This section describes the project that we will improve on, as we go through the following three chapters – the *Comic Creator*. The basic idea of the project is a simple application to draw a stickman. The following screenshot is a sketch (wireframe) of the GUI we are aiming for:

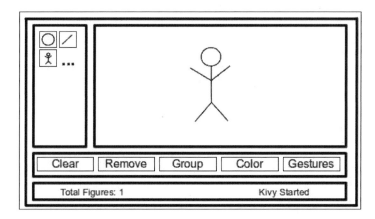

We can distinguish several areas in the sketch. First, we need a *drawing space* (top-right) for our comics. We need a *tool box* (top-left) with some drawing tools to draw our figures and also some *general options* (second from bottom to top) – clear the screen, remove the last element, group elements, change color, and use the gestures mode. Finally, it would be useful to have a *status bar* (center-bottom) to provide some information to the user – number of figures and last action performed. According to what we have learned in this chapter, there are multiple solutions to organize this screen. We will use the following:

- AnchorLayout for the *tool box* area in the top-left corner. Inside it will be a GridLayout of two columns for the *drawing tools*.

- AnchorLayout for the *drawing space* in the top-right corner. Inside it will be a RelativeLayout to have a relative space to draw in.

- AnchorLayout for the *general options* and *status bar* area at the bottom. Inside it will be a BoxLayout with vertical orientation to organize the *general options* on top of the *status bar*:

  - BoxLayout with horizontal orientation for the buttons of the *general options*.

  - BoxLayout with horizontal orientation for the labels of the *status bar*.

We are going to use that structure by creating different files for each area – `comiccreator.py`, `comiccreator.kv`, `toolbox.kv`, `generaltools.kv`, `drawingspace.kv`, and `statusbar.kv`. Let's start with `comiccreator.py`:

```
198. # File name: comiccreator.py
199. from kivy.app import App
200. from kivy.lang import Builder
201. from kivy.uix.anchorlayout import AnchorLayout
200.
201. Builder.load_file('toolbox.kv')
202. Builder.load_file('drawingspace.kv')
203. Builder.load_file('generaloptions.kv')
204. Builder.load_file('statusbar.kv')
205.
206. class ComicCreator(AnchorLayout):
207.     pass
208.
209. class ComicCreatorApp(App):
210. def build(self):
211.         return ComicCreator()
212.
213. if __name__=="__main__":
214.     ComicCreatorApp().run()
```

Note that we are explicitly loading some of the files with the `Builder.load_file` instruction (lines 203 to 206). There is no need to explicitly load `comiccreator.kv` because Kivy automatically loads it by extracting the first part of the `ComicCreatorApp` name. For `ComicCreator`, we choose `AnchorLayout`. It is not the only option, but it gives clarity to the code, because the second level is also composed of `AnchorLayout` instances.

Even though using a simple widget would have been clear, it is not possible, because the `Widget` class doesn't honor the `size_hint` and `pos_hint` properties that are necessary in the `AnchorLayout` internals.

 Remember that only layouts honor the `size_hint` and `pos_hint` properties.

Here is the code for comiccreator.kv:

```
216.  # File name: comiccreator.kv
217.  <ComicCreator>:
218.      AnchorLayout:
219.          anchor_x: 'left'
220.          anchor_y: 'top'
221.          ToolBox:
222.              id: _tool_box
223.              size_hint: None, None
224.              width: 100
225.      AnchorLayout:
226.          anchor_x: 'right'
227.          anchor_y: 'top'
228.          DrawingSpace:
229.              size_hint: None, None
230.              width: root.width - _tool_box.width
231.              height: root.height - _general_options.height -
                      _status_bar.height
232.      AnchorLayout:
233.          anchor_x: 'center'
234.          anchor_y: 'bottom'
235.          BoxLayout:
236.              orientation: 'vertical'
237.              GeneralOptions:
238.                  id: _general_options
239.                  size_hint: 1,None
240.                  height: 48
241.              StatusBar:
242.                  id: _status_bar
243.                  size_hint: 1,None
244.                  height: 24
```

This code follows the previously presented structure for the *Comic Creator*. There are basically three AnchorLayout instances in the first level (lines 219, 226, and 233) and a BoxLayout that organizes the *general options* and the *status bar* (line 236).

We set the width of the ToolBox to 100 pixels and the height of the GeneralOptions and StatusBar to 48 and 24 pixels respectively (lines 241 and 245). This brings with it an interesting problem – the *drawing space* should use the remaining width and height of the screen (no matter the screen size). In order to achieve this, we will take advantage of the Kivy **id** (lines 223, 239, and 243), which allows us to refer to other components inside the Kivy language. On lines 231 and 232, we subtract tool_box. width from root.width (line 231) and general_options.height and status_bar. height from root.height (line 232).

A Kivy **id** allows us to create internal variables in order to access properties of other widgets inside the Kivy language rules.

For now, let's continue exploring the Kivy language in the toolbox.kv:

```
245. # File name: toolbox.kv
246. <ToolButton@ToggleButton>:
247.     size_hint: None, None
248.     size: 48,48
249.     group: 'tool'
250.
251. <ToolBox@GridLayout>:
252.     cols: 2
253.     padding: 2
254.     ToolButton:
255.         text: 'O'
256.     ToolButton:
257.         text: '/'
258.     ToolButton:
259.         text: '?'
```

We created a ToolButton class that defines the size of the drawing tools and also introduces a new Kivy widget – **ToggleButton**. The difference with the normal Button is that it stays pressed until we click on it again. The following is an example of the *tool box* with a ToolButton activated:

A ToggleButton instance can be associated with other ToggleButton instances, so just one of them is clicked on at a time. We can achieve this by assigning the same **group** property (line 250) to the ToggleButton instances that we want to react together. In this case, we want all the instances of ToolButton belonging to the same group, because we want to draw just one figure at a time; we make it part of the class definition (line 247).

On line 252, we implement ToolBox as a subclass of GridLayout and we add some character placeholders ('O', '/', and '?') to the ToolButton instances that we will substitute for something more appropriate in the following chapters.

The following is the code for generaloptions.kv:

```
260. # File name: generaloptions.kv
261. <GeneralOptions@BoxLayout>:
262.     orientation: 'horizontal'
263.     padding: 2
264.     Button:
265.         text: 'Clear'
266.     Button:
267.         text: 'Remove'
268.     ToggleButton:
269.         text: 'Group'
268.     Button:
270.         text: 'Color'
271.     ToggleButton:
272.         text: 'Gestures'
```

Here is an example of how inheritance can help us separate our components. We are using `ToggleButton` instances (lines 269 and 273), and they are not affected by the previous `ToolButton` implementation. Also, we didn't associate them to any `group`, so they are independent of each other and will just keep a mode or state. The code only defines the `GeneralOptions` class following our initial structure. The following is the resulting screenshot:

The `statusbar.kv` file is very similar in the way it uses `BoxLayout`:

```
274. # File name: statusbar.kv
275. <StatusBar@BoxLayout>:
276.     orientation: 'horizontal'
277.     Label:
278.         text: 'Total Figures: ?'
279.     Label:
280.         text: "Kivy started"
```

The difference is that it organizes labels and not buttons. The following is the screenshot:

Finally, the code for `drawingspace.kv`:

```
281. # File name: drawingspace.kv
282. <DrawingSpace@RelativeLayout>:
283.     Label:
284.         markup: True
285.         text: '[size=32px][color=#3e6643]The[/color]
                [sub]Comic[/sub] [i][b]Creator[/b][/i][/size]'
```

Apart from defining that `DrawingSpace` is a subclass of `RelativeLayout`, we introduce the Kivy **markup**, a nice feature for styling the text of the `Label` class. It works in a similar manner to XML-based languages. For example, in HTML, `<b>I am bold</b>` would specify bold text. First, you have to activate it (line 285) and then you just embed the text you want to style between `[tag]` and `[/tag]` (line 286). You can find the complete tag list and description in the Kivy API, in the documentation for `Label` (`http://kivy.org/docs/api-kivy.uix.label.html`). In the previous example, `size` and `color` are self-explanatory; `sub` refers to subindexed text; `b` to bold; and `i` to italics.

Here is the screenshot that shows the GUI of our project:

In the following chapters, we are going to add the respective functionality to this interface that, for now, consists of placeholder widgets. However, it is exciting what we got with just a few lines of code. Our GUI is ready to go and we will be working on its logic from now on.

Summary

This chapter covered all the basics and introduced some not-so-basic concepts of Kivy. We covered how to configure classes, instances, and templates. Here is a list of Kivy elements we have learned to use in this chapter:

- Basic widgets – `Widget`, `Button`, `ToggleButton`, and `Label`
- Layouts – `FloatLayout`, `RelativeLayout`, `BoxLayout`, `GridLayout`, `StackLayout`, `AnchorLayout`, and `PageLayout`
- Properties – `pos`, `x`, `y`, `center_x`, `center_y`, `top`, `right`, `size`, `height`, `width`, `pos_hint`, `size_hint`, `group`, `spacing`, `padding`, `color`, `text`, `font_size`, `cols`, `rows`, `orientation`, `anchor_x`, and `anchor_y`
- Variables – `self` and `root`
- Others – `id` and the markup tags `size`, `color`, `b`, `i`, and `sub`

There are many more elements from the Kivy language that we can use, but with this chapter, we have understood the general idea of how to organize elements. With the help of the Kivy API, we should be able to display most of the elements available for GUI design. There is, however, a very important element we need to study separately – the `canvas`, which allows us to draw vector shapes inside widgets, such as the white rectangle we draw as background in the `PageLayout` example. It is a very important topic to master in Kivy, and the entire next chapter, *Graphics - The Canvas*, will be dedicated to it.

2
Graphics – the Canvas

Any Kivy `Widget` contains a **Canvas** object. A Kivy **Canvas** is a set of drawing instructions that define the graphical representation of `Widget`.

 Be careful with the name because it tends to be confusing! A **Canvas** object is not what we draw on (for example, as it is in HTML5); it is a set of instructions to draw in the **coordinate space**.

The coordinate space refers to the place in which we draw. All the Kivy widgets share the same coordinate space, and a `Canvas` instance, the instructions to draw on it. A coordinate space is not restricted to the size of the window or the application screen, which means that we can draw outside of the visible area.

We will discuss how to draw and manipulate the representation of the widgets through the instructions we add to the `Canvas` object. Here is a list of the most important skills that we will cover:

- Drawing basic geometric shapes (straight and curve lines, ellipses, and polygons) through **vertex instructions**
- Using colors, and rotating, translating, and scaling the coordinate space through the **context instructions**
- The difference between vertex and context instructions and how they complement each other
- The three different sets of instructions of `Canvas` that we can use to modify the order of execution of the graphics instructions
- Storing and retrieving the current coordinate space context through `PushMatrix` and `PopMatrix`

Using the Kivy canvas brings with it some technical challenges because Kivy integrates graphic processing with efficiency in mind. These challenges are not initially obvious, but there is nothing particularly difficult about them if we understand the underlying problem. This is why the next section is dedicated to introduce the main considerations that we face when we use the canvas.

Understanding the canvas

Before studying the examples of this chapter, it is important to recapitulate the following particularities related to the graphics display:

- The coordinate space refers to the place in which we draw, which is not restricted to the windows size

- A Canvas object is a set of instructions to draw in the coordinate space, not the place we draw in

- All Widget objects contain their own Canvas (canvases, which we will see later) but all of them share the same coordinate space, the one in the App object.

For example, if we add a rotation instruction to a specific Canvas instance (for example, the canvas of a button), then this will also affect all the subsequent graphics instructions that are going to display graphics in the coordinate space. It doesn't matter if the graphics belong to canvases of different widgets; they all share the same coordinate space.

Therefore, we need to learn techniques to leave the coordinate space context in its original state after modifying it with graphics instructions.

All the graphics instructions added to different Canvas objects, which at the same time belong to different Widget objects, affect the same coordinate space. It is our task to make sure that the coordinate space is in its original state after modifying it with the graphics instructions.

Another important concept that we need to extend is the one of the **Widget**. We already know that widgets are the blocks that allow us to build interfaces.

A `Widget` is also a place marker (with its position and size), but not necessarily a placeholder. The instructions of the canvas of a widget are not restricted to the specific area of the widget but to the whole coordinate space.

This directly adds to the previous problem of sharing a coordinate space. Not only do we need to control the fact that we share a coordinate space, but also, we have no restrictions on where to draw. On one hand, this makes Kivy very efficient and gives us a lot of flexibility. On the other hand, this seems to be a lot to control. Fortunately, Kivy provides the necessary tools to easily work around the problem.

The next section will present the available graphics instructions that can be added to the canvas in order to draw basic shapes. After this, we will explore graphic instructions that change the coordinate space context and exemplify the problems of sharing the coordinate space. The final section concentrates on illustrating the acquired knowledge inside the **Comic Creator**, where we learn the most common techniques to master the use of the canvas considering its particularities. By the end of this chapter, we will be in complete control of the graphics that are displayed on the screen.

Drawing basic shapes

Before starting, let's introduce the Python code that we will reuse in all the examples of this chapter:

```
1. # File name: drawing.py
2. from kivy.app import App
3. from kivy.uix.relativelayout import RelativeLayout
4.
5. class DrawingSpace(RelativeLayout):
6.     pass
7.
8. class DrawingApp(App):
9.     def build(self):
10.         return DrawingSpace()
11.
12. if __name__=="__main__":
13.     DrawingApp().run()
```

We created the subclass `DrawingSpace` from `RelativeLayout`. It could have been inherited from any `Widget` but using `RelativeLayout` is generally a good choice for graphics because we usually want to draw inside the widget, and that means relative to its position.

Let's start with the canvas. There are basically two types of instructions that we can add to a canvas: vertex instructions and context instructions.

> The **vertex instructions** inherit from the **`VertexInstruction`** base class, and allow us to draw vector shapes in the coordinate space.
>
> The **context instructions** (`Color`, `Rotate`, `Translate`, and `Scale`) inherit from the **`ContextInstruction`** base class, and let us apply transformations to the **coordinate space context**. By **coordinate space context**, we mean the conditions in which the shapes (specified in the vertex instructions) are drawn in the coordinate space.

Basically, **vertex instructions** are what we draw and **context instructions** affect where and how we draw. The following is the screenshot for the first example of this chapter:

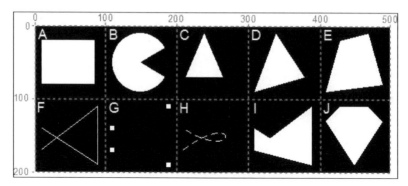

In the preceding screenshot, the gray grid will simplify reading the coordinates that appear in the code. Also, the white letters associated with each cell will be used to refer to the shapes. Neither the grid nor the letters are part of the Kivy example. The preceding screenshot illustrates 10 basic figures that we learn to draw with vertex instructions. Almost all the available Kivy classes are represented in this example and we can create any 2D geometric shape with them. Since the vertex instructions use fixed coordinates, it is important to run this example with a screen size of 500 x 200 (`python drawing.py --size=500x200`) in order to visualize the shapes correctly.

We will study the Kivy language (`drawing.kv`) with small code fragments associated to the respective figure (and coordinates) next to it, so it would be easier to follow. Let's start with the shape **A** (rectangle):

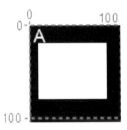

Following is the code snippet for shape **A**:

```
14. # File name: drawing.kv (vertex instructions)
15. <DrawingSpace>:
16.     canvas:
17.         Rectangle:
18.             pos: self.x+10,self.top-80
19.             size: self.width*0.15, self.height*0.3
```

Rectangle is a good starting point because it resembles the way we set properties in widgets. We just have to set the **pos** and **size** properties.

> The **pos** and **size** properties of the vertex instructions are different from the pos and size properties of `Widget`, since they belong to the `VertexInstruction` base class. All the values to specify the properties of the vertex instructions are given in fixed values.

This means that we cannot use the `size_hint` or `pos_hint` properties as we did with the widgets in *Chapter 1, GUI Basics – Building an Interface*. However, we can use the properties of `self` to achieve similar results (Line 18 and 19).

Let's proceed with the shape **B** (Pac-Man-like figure):

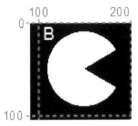

Following is the code snippet for shape **B**:

```
20.              Ellipse:
21.                  angle_start: 120
22.                  angle_end: 420
23.                  pos: 110, 110
24.                  size: 80,80
```

The **Ellipse** works very similar to `Rectangle`, but it has three new properties: **angle_start**, **angle_end**, and **segments**. The first two properties specify the initial and final angle of the ellipse. The angle 0° is North (or 12 o'clock) and they add up in the clockwise direction. So, the `angle_start` is 120° (90° + 30°), which is the lower jaw of the Pac-Man-like figure (Line 21). The `angle_end` value is 420° (360° + (90°-30°)), which is bigger than `angle_start` because we need Kivy to follow the clockwise direction to paint the `Ellipse`. If we specify a lower value than `angle_start`, Kivy will follow a counter clockwise direction, painting where the mouth of the Pac-Man is, instead of its body.

Let's continue with the shape C (triangle):

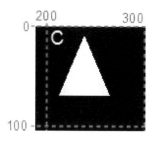

```
25.              Ellipse:
26.                  segments: 3
27.                  pos: 210,110
28.                  size: 60,80
```

The triangle of shape **C** is actually another **Ellipse** that we obtain thanks to the **segments** property (Line 26). Let's put it this way: if you have to draw an ellipse with three lines, the best you would end up with is a triangle. If you have four lines, you would end up with a rectangle. You actually need infinite lines for a perfect `Ellipse`, but a computer cannot process that (neither the screen has enough resolution to support this), so we need to stop at some point. The default `segments` are 180. Notice that if you have a circle (that is, size: x,x), you will always get equilateral polygons (for example, a square if you specify just four `segments`).

We can analyze shapes **D**, **E**, **F**, and **G** together:

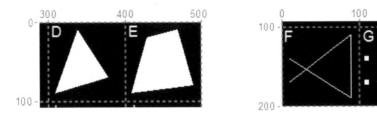

```
29.          Triangle:
30.              points: 310,110,340,190,380,130
31.           Quad:
32.              points: 410,110,430,180,470,190,490,120
33.           Line:
34.              points: 10,30, 90,90, 90,10, 10,60
35.           Point:
36.              points: 110,30, 190,90, 190,10, 110,60
37.              pointsize: 3
```

Triangle (shape **D**), **Quad** (shape **E**), and **Line** (shape **F**) work similarly.
Their **points** property (Lines 30, 32, and 34) indicates the corners of a triangle,
quadrilateral, and a line, respectively. The **points** property is a sequence of
coordinates in the format (x1, y1, x2, y2). Point is also similar to these three
shapes. It uses the **points** property (Line 36) but in this case to indicate a sequence
of points (shape **G**). It also uses the **pointsize** (Line 37) property to indicate the
size of the Points.

Let's proceed with the shape **H**:

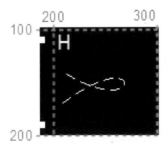

```
38.          Bezier:
39.              points: 210,30, 290,90, 290,10, 210,60
40.              segments: 360
41.             dash_length: 10
42.             dash_offset: 5
```

Bezier is a curved line that uses the **points** property as a set of 'attractors' of the curve line (there is a math formalism behind Bézier curves that we are not going to cover in this book because it is out of its scope, but you can find enough information in Wikipedia http://en.wikipedia.org/wiki/Bézier_curve). The points are attractors because the line does not touch all of them (just the first and the last of them). The points of Bezier (Line 39) are at the same distance from each other as the points of the Line (Line 34), or the Point (Line 36); they were just translated 100 pixels to the right. You can visually compare the result of the Bezier curve (shape **H**), with the results of the Line (shape **G**) or the Point (shape **H**). We included two other properties **dash_length** (Line 41), for the length of the dashes of the discontinuous line, and **dash_offset** (Line 42) for the distance between the dashes.

Let's cover the last shapes **I** and **J**:

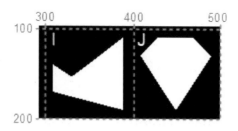

```
43.         Mesh:
44.             mode: 'triangle_fan'
45.             vertices: 310,30,0,0,  390,90,0,0,  390,10,0,0,
                    310,60,0,0
46.             indices: 0,1,2,3
47.         Mesh:
48.             mode: 'triangle_fan'
49.             vertices: 430,90,0,0,  470,90,0,0,  490,70,0,0,
                    450,10,0,0,  410,70,0,0,  430,90,0,0,
50.             indices: 0,1,2,3,4,5
```

We added two **Mesh** instructions (Lines 43 and 47). A **Mesh** instruction is a compound of triangles and has many applications in computer graphics and games. There is not enough space in this book to cover the advanced techniques to use this instruction, but at the very least we will understand its basics and be able to draw flat polygons. The **mode** property is set to triangle_fan (Line 44), which means that the triangles of the mesh are filled with color, instead of, for example, just drawing the border.

The **vertices** property is a tuple of coordinates. For the purpose of this example, we will just ignore all the 0s. This will leave us with four coordinates (or vertices) in line 45. These points are relatively the same as shapes **F**, **G**, and **H**. Let's imagine for the shape I how the triangles are created as we traverse them, left to right on the vertex list using three vertex points each time. The shape **I** is composed of two triangles. The first triangle uses the first, second, and third vertices; and the second triangle uses the first, third, and fourth vertices. In general, if we are in the ith vertex of the list, a triangle is drawn using the first vertex, the $(i-1)^{th}$ vertex, and the ith vertex. The final mesh (shape **J**) presents another example. It contains three triangles that are surrounded by a blue line in the following screenshot:

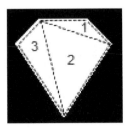

The **indexes** property contains a list with the same number of vertices (not counting the 0s) and instructs the order in which the vertices list is traversed, altering the triangles that compose the mesh.

So far, all the polygons that we studied have been colored in. If we need to draw the border of the polygon, we should use **Line** instead. In principle, this seems easy for a basic shape such as a triangle, but how do we draw a circle with just points? Fortunately, Line has the appropriate properties to make things easier.

The next example will show how you can build the figures in the following screenshot:

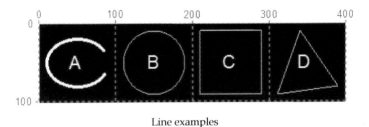

Line examples

We have kept the gray coordinates and the letter to identify each cell in the screenshot. The Python code should be run in a screen size of 400 x 100: `python drawing.py --size=400x100`. The following is the `drawing.kv` code for the previous screenshot:

```
51. # File name: drawing.kv (Line Examples)
52. <DrawingSpace>:
53.     canvas:
54.         Line:
55.             ellipse: 10, 20, 80, 60, 120, 420, 180
56.             width: 2
57.         Line:
58.             circle: 150, 50, 40, 0, 360, 180
59.         Line:
60.             rectangle: 210,10,80,80
61.         Line:
62.             points: 310,10,340,90,390,20
63.             close: True
```

In the previous code, we added four **Line** instructions using specific properties. The first `Line` instruction (in line 54, shape **A**) is similar to our Pac-Man (line 20). The **ellipse** property (line 55) specifies x, y, width, height, angle_start, angle_end, and segments, respectively. The order of the parameters is difficult to remember so we should always keep the Kivy API next to us (http://kivy.org/docs/api-kivy.graphics.vertex_instructions.html). We also set **width** of Line to make it thicker (line 56).

The second `Line` instruction (line 57, shape **B**) introduces a property that has no counterpart in the vertex instructions: **circle**. The difference with the ellipse property is that the first three parameters (line 58) define the center (150, 50) and radius (40) of Circle. The rest remains the same. The third `Line` (line 59, shape **C**) is defined by **rectangle** (line 60) and the parameters are simply x, y, width, and height. The last `Line` (line 61, shape **D**) is the most flexible way to define polygons. We specified the points (line 62), as many as we want. The **close** property (line 63) connects the first and last points.

We covered most of the instructions and properties related to vertex instructions. We should be able to draw any geometrical shape in two dimensions with Kivy. If you want more details about each of the instructions, you should visit the Kivy API (http://kivy.org/docs/api-kivy.graphics.vertex_instructions.html). Now, it is the turn of context instructions to decorate these boring black and white polygons.

Adding images, colors, and backgrounds

In this section, we will discuss how to add images and colors to our graphics and how to control which graphic comes on top of which one. We continue using the same Python code of the first section. This time, we run it with a 400 x 100 screen size: `python drawing.py --size=400x100`. The following screenshot shows the final result of this section:

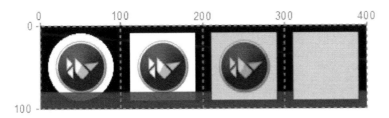

Images and Colors

The following is the corresponding `drawing.kv` code:

```
64. # File name: drawing.kv (Images and colors)
65. <DrawingSpace>:
66.     canvas:
67.         Ellipse:
68.             pos: 10,10
69.             size: 80,80
70.             source: 'kivy.png'
71.         Rectangle:
72.             pos: 110,10
73.             size: 80,80
74.             source: 'kivy.png'
75.         Color:
76.             rgba: 0,0,1,.75
77.         Line:
78.             points: 10,10,390,10
79.             width: 10
80.             cap: 'square'
81.         Color:
82.             rgba: 0,1,0,1
83.         Rectangle:
84.             pos: 210,10
85              size: 80,80
86.             source: 'kivy.png'
87.         Rectangle:
88.             pos: 310,10
89.             size: 80,80
```

This code starts with Ellipse (line 67) and Rectangle (line 71). We used the **source** property, which inserts an image to decorate each polygon. The kivy.png image is 80 x 80 pixels with a white background (without any alpha/transparency channel). The result is shown in the first two columns of the "Images and Colors" screenshot.

In line 75, we used the context instruction **Color** to change the color (with the **rgba** property: red, green, blue, and alpha) of the coordinate space context. This means that the next vertex instruction will be drawn with the color changed by rgba. A context instruction basically changes the current coordinate space context. In the screenshot, you can see the thin blue bar (or very dark gray bar in the printed version of this book) at the bottom (line 77) that appears as transparent blue (line 76) instead of the default white (1,1,1,1) of the previous examples. We set the ends shape of the line, to a square with the **cap** property (line 80).

We changed the color again in line 81. After this, we drew two more rectangles, one with the kivy.png image and another without it. In the preceding screenshot, you can see that the white part of the image has become as green, or light gray in the printed version of this book, as the basic Rectangle on the right.

> The Color instruction acts as a light that illuminates the kivy.png image, it doesn't simply paint over it.

There is another important detail to notice in the screenshot. The blue (dark gray in the printed version) line at the bottom goes over the first two polygons and goes under the last two. The instructions are executed in order and this might bring some unwanted results. Kivy provides a solution to make this execution more flexible, and structured, which we will introduce in the next section.

Structuring graphic instructions

Apart from the canvas instance, a Widget includes two other canvas instances: **canvas.before** and **canvas.after**.

> The Widget class has three sets of instructions (**canvas.before, canvas,** and **canvas.after**) to organize the order of execution. With them, we can control which elements will go to the background or stay on the foreground.

The following `drawing.kv` file shows an example of these three sets (lines 92, 98, and 104) of instructions:

```
90.  # File name: drawing.kv (Before and After Canvas)
91.  <DrawingSpace>:
92.      canvas.before:
93.          Color:
94.              rgba: 1,0,0,1
95.          Rectangle:
96.              pos: 0,0
97.              size: 100,100
98.      canvas:
99.          Color:
100.             rgba: 0,1,0,1
101.         Rectangle:
102.             pos: 100,0
103.             size: 100,100
104.     canvas.after:
105.         Color:
106.             rgba: 0,0,1,1
107.         Rectangle:
108.             pos: 200,0
109.             size: 100,100
110.     Button:
111.         text: 'A very very very long button'
112.         pos_hint: {'center_x': .5, 'center_y': .5}
113.         size_hint: .9,.1
```

In each set, a rectangle of different color is drawn (lines 95, 101, and 107). Here is a diagram that illustrates the execution order of the canvases. The numbers on the top-left margin of each code block indicates the order of execution:

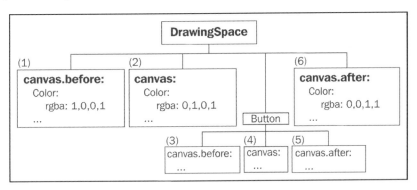

Execution order of the canvas

Notice that we didn't define any `canvas`, `canvas.before`, or `canvas.after` for `Button` but Kivy does internally. Since `Button` displays graphics on the screen (for example, it contains `Rectangle` associated with the **background_color** property), then it has instructions in its canvas sets. The final result is shown in the following screenshot (executed with: `python drawing.py --size=300x100`):

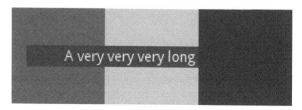

Before and after canvas

The graphics of `Button` (the child) are covered up by the set of instructions in `canvas.after`. It is clear that the instructions of `canvas.before` and `canvas` are executed before the displaying `Button`, but what is executed between them? It is necessary when we work with inheritance, and we want to add instructions in the subclass that should be executed before the `canvas` set of instructions of the base class. Also, it is a convenience when we mix Python code and Kivy language rules. We will study some practical examples in the last section of this chapter related to the *Comic Creator*, and review the topic in *Chapter 4, Improving the User Experience*.

For now, it is good enough to understand that we have three sets of instructions (`Canvas`) that provide some flexibility when we display graphics on the screen. Let's now explore some more context instructions related to transformations of the vertex instruction.

Rotating, translating, and scaling the coordinate space

`Rotate`, `Translate`, and `Scale` are context instructions that are applied to the vertex instructions, which are displayed in the coordinate space. They could bring unexpected results if we forget that the coordinate space is shared among all widgets, and it occupies the size of the window (actually bigger than that because there is no restriction on the coordinates and we can draw outside the window). First, we are going to understand the behavior of this instruction in this section and, in the next section, we can analyze the problems they bring in a deeper way, and learn techniques to make things easier.

Let's start with the new drawing.kv code:

```
114. # File name: drawing.kv (Rotate, Translate and Scale)
115. <DrawingSpace>:
116.    pos_hint: {'x':.5, 'y':.5}
117.    canvas:
118.        Rectangle:
119.            source: 'kivy.png'
120.        Rotate:
121.            angle: 90
122.            axis: 0,0,1
123.        Color:
124.            rgb: 1,0,0 # Red color
125.        Rectangle:
126.            source: 'kivy.png'
127.        Translate:
128.            x: -100
129.        Color:
130.            rgb: 0,1,0 # Green color
131.        Rectangle:
132.            source: 'kivy.png'
133.        Translate:
134.            y: -100
135.        Scale:
136.            xyz:(.5,.5,0)
137.        Color:
138.            rgb: 0,0,1 # Blue color
139.        Rectangle:
140.            source: 'kivy.png'
```

In this code, the first thing we did is position the coordinates (0, 0) of DrawingSpace (RelativeLayout) in the center of the screen (line 116). We created Rectangle with the kivi.png figure, which we had previously modified to indicate the original **x** axis and **y** axis.

The result is presented in the top-right of the following screenshot (executed with
`python drawing.py --size=200x200`):

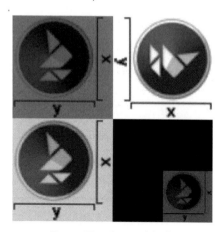

Rotate, Translate and Scale

In the line 120, we applied the **Rotate** instruction by 90° on the z axis (line 122).
The value is (x, y, z), which means we can use any vector in the 3D space. Think
of this as nailing a pin to the bottom-left corner of `DrawingSpace`, which we then
rotate in the counter clockwise direction.

 By default, the pin nail of the rotation is always the coordinates (0, 0)
but we can alter this behavior with the **origin** property.

The top-left section of the screenshot ("Rotate, Translate, and Scale") shows the
result after the rotation. We drew the same rectangle with red color (using the **rgb**
property instead of the `rgba` property) to highlight it. After adding a rotation to the
coordinate space context, we also modified the relative X-axis and Y-axis. Line 128
considers that the axes are rotated, and in order to translate the coordinate space
down (usually Y-axis), it sets -100px to the X-axis. We drew the same `Rectangle`
with green `Color` in the bottom left corner. Notice that the image still rotates and it
will rotate as long as we don't bring the coordinate space context to its original angle.

 Context instructions are persistent until we change them
back again. Another way to avoid this is working inside
`RelativeLayout`. If you remember from the previous chapter,
it allows us to work with coordinates relative to the widget.

To scale or zoom out the image, we translated the coordinate space context (line 133) to use the bottom-right section of the screenshot. Notice that we use the Y-axis instead of the X-axis, since the context is still rotated. The scaling is done in line 135, where the image will be reduced to half the width and half the height. The `Scale` instruction reduces towards the (0, 0) coordinate, which initially is at the bottom-left corner. However, after all these modifications of the context, we need to think where this coordinate is. First, we rotated the axis (line 120) so the X-axis is vertical and the Y-axis is horizontal. After translating the coordinate space down (line 127) and then right (line 133), the (0, 0) coordinate is in the bottom-right corner with the X-axis being the vertical one and the Y-axis being the horizontal one.

 `Scale` uses proportions to the current size of the coordinate space context and not the original size. For example, to recover the original size, we should use `xyz: (2,2,0)` and not just `xyz: (1,1,0)`.

So far, in this chapter, we have discussed that a `Canvas` instance is a set of instructions that contains context instructions and vertex instructions. The context instructions apply changes (colors or transformation) to the coordinate space context that affects the conditions in which the vertex instructions are displayed in the coordinate space.

We will use some of the knowledge to add *Stickman* to our project in the next and final section of this chapter. We will introduce two important context instructions to deal with the issues of sharing the same coordinate space between widgets: `PushMatrix` and `PopMatrix`.

Comic Creator: PushMatrix and PopMatrix

Let's insert some graphics to the project we started in *Chapter 1, GUI Basics – Building an Interface*. Before this, we need to recapitulate two important lessons of this chapter related to the coordinate space:

- The coordinate space is not restricted to any position or size. It normally has its origin in the bottom-left corner of the screen. To avoid this, we use `RelativeLayout`, which internally performs a translation to the position of the `Widget`.

- Once the coordinate space context is transformed by any instruction, it stays like that until we specify something different. `RelativeLayout` also addresses this problem with two contextual instructions, which we will study in this section: **PushMatrix** and **PopMatrix**.

We use `RelativeLayout` in this section to avoid the problems of the shared coordinate space, but we will also explain the alternatives to it when we are inside any other type of `Widget`. We will add a new file (`comicwidgets.kv`) to our project. In `comicreator.py`, we need to add our new file to `Builder`:

```
Builder.load_file('comicwidgets.kv')
```

The file `comicwidgets.kv` will contain special widgets, which we will create for the project. In this chapter, we will add the `StickMan` class:

```
141. # File name: comicwidgets.kv
142. <StickMan@RelativeLayout>:
143.     size_hint: None, None
144.     size: 48,48
145.     canvas:
146.         PushMatrix
147.         Line:
148.             circle: 24,38,5
149.         Line:
150.             points: 24,33,24,15
151.         Line:
152.             points: 14,5,24,15
153.         Line:
154.             points: 34,5,24,15
155.         Translate:
156.             y: 48-8
157.         Rotate:
158.             angle: 180
159.             axis: 1,0,0
160.         Line:
161.             points: 14,5,24,15
162.         Line:
163.             points: 34,5,24,15
164.         PopMatrix
```

On line 142, the StickMan subclass inherits from RelativeLayout to facilitate the positioning and use of context instructions. We defined StickMan of size 48 x 48. StickMan is composed of six lines that define the head, body, left leg, right leg, left arm, and right arm (line 147 to 163). You can see the result of StickMan three times in the following screenshot:

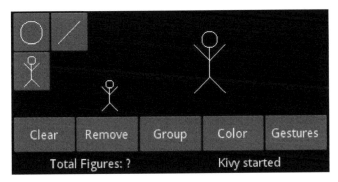

Comic Creator

The first StickMan is part of the design of the last ToolButton and the other two appear in the *drawing space*; one of them is scaled. Notice that the code of the legs (lines 151 to 154) is exactly the same as the arms (lines 160 to 163); the difference is that we translated the coordinate space upwards (lines 155 and 156) and rotated it 180° in the x-axis (lines 157 to 159). With this, we saved ourselves some math to draw the *stickman*.

We translated and rotated the coordinate space context; therefore, we should undo these context changes so everything will remain as it was at the beginning. Instead of adding more instructions to Translate and Rotate back to the coordinate space context, we used two convenient Kivy instructions: **PushMatrix** and **PopMatrix**. At the beginning, we used a PushMatrix (line 146), which will save the current coordinate space context and, at the end, we used a PopMatrix (line 164) to return the context to its original state.

PushMatrix saves the current coordinate space context and **PopMatrix** retrieves the last saved coordinate space context. Therefore, the transformation instructions (Scale, Rotate, and Translate) surrounded by **PushMatrix** and **PopMatrix** won't affect the rest of the interface.

We will extend this approach to add shapes to the other two instances of ToolButton (circle and line) in the top-left corner of ToolBox. We add this code in toolbox.kv:

```
165. # File name: toolbox.kv
166. <ToolButton@ToggleButton>:
167.     size_hint: None,None
168.     size: 48,48
169.     group: 'tool'
170.     canvas:
171.         PushMatrix:
172.         Translate:
173.             xy: self.x,self.y
174.     canvas.after:
175.         PopMatrix:
176.
177. <ToolBox@GridLayout>:
178.     cols: 2
179.     padding: 2
180.     ToolButton:
181.         canvas:
182.             Line:
183.                 circle: 24,24,14
184.     ToolButton:
185.         canvas:
186.             Line:
187.                 points: 10,10,38,38
188.     ToolButton:
189.         StickMan:
190.             pos_hint: {'center_x':.5,'center_y':.5}
```

In the `ToolButton` class (line 166), we used a `PushMatrix` (line 171) in the `canvas` set of instructions to save the current state of the coordinate space. Then, `Translate` (line 172) moves the graphic instructions to the position of `ToolButton` so we can use relative coordinates on each `ToolButton` (line 180 to 190). Finally, `PopMatrix` (line 175) was added to `canvas.after` to restore the coordinate space.

It is important to follow the execution order of the different canvases (instruction sets). For example, let's slowly follow the execution order of the canvases of `ToolButton` that contains the circle (line 180): first, `canvas` of the `ToolButton` class that has `PushMatrix` and `Translate` (line 170); second, `canvas` of the `ToolButton` instance, which has the circle (line 181), and third, `canvas.after` of the base class, which has `PopMatrix` (line 174). We just implemented the same technique used for `RelativeLayout`.

> `RelativeLayout` internally contains `PushMatrix` and `PopMatrix`. Therefore, we can add instructions safely inside it, which won't affect the rest of the interface.

Let's conclude this chapter by scaling our *stickman* in the *drawing space* and illustrate one more particularity of the execution order of the canvases. The following is the code of `drawingspace.kv`:

```
191. # File name: drawingspace.kv
192. <DrawingSpace@RelativeLayout>:
193.     StickMan:
194.         pos_hint: {'center_x':.5,'center_y':.5}
195.         canvas.before:
196.             Translate:
197.                 xy: -self.width/2, -self.height/2
198.             Scale:
199.                 xyz: 2,2,0
200.     StickMan:
```

The first StickMan was translated and rotated (lines 193 to 199), but not the second one (line 200). We discussed that the context instructions affect the coordinate space globally, but when we see the result in the screenshot ("Comic Creator"), we realize that the second instance was neither scaled nor translated by the lines 196 and 198. What happened? The answer is not obvious. Is the answer related to PushMatrix and PopMatrix inside the canvas of the StickMan class (lines 146 and 164)? No, it isn't, because both of them are inside the same set of instructions.

The way we implemented ToolButton follows the way the RelativeLayout class is implemented. StickMan inherits from RelativeLayout, so there is actually another PushMatrix in canvas.before and its respective PopMatrix in canvas.after of the StickMan class (inherited from RelativeLayout). The instructions from lines 196 to 199 are executed after PopMatrix is executed in canvas.before of RelativeLayout and, therefore, the context is restored on the respective PushMatrix of RelativeLayout.

Finally, notice that the instructions must be in canvas.before because they are added before the existent instructions, the ones that actually draw the *stickman*. In other words, if we simply add them in the canvas, then the *stickman* would be drawn before the translation and scaling.

The rest of the files of the *Comic Creator* comiccreator.kv, generaloptions.kv, and statusbar.kv were not modified, so we are not presenting them again. The context and vertex instructions are easy to understand. However, we must be very careful with the order of execution and make sure to leave the coordinate space context in its normal state after executing the desired vertex instructions. Finally, take into account that everything you see in the screen is displayed by an instruction (or instructions) inside the canvas, including, for example, Label texts and the Button backgrounds.

Summary

This chapter explained the necessary concepts to understand the use of the canvas. We covered the use of vertex and context instructions, and how to manipulate the order of the execution of instructions. We covered how to deal with the transformation of canvas, either reversing all the transformations or using RelativeLayout. The following is the whole set of components we learnt to use, in this chapter:

- The vertex instructions (and many of their respective properties): Rectangle (pos, size), Ellipse (pos, size, angle_start, angle_end, segments), Triangle (points), Quad (points), Point (points, pointsize), Line (points, ellipse, circle, rectangle, width, close, dash_lenght, dash_offset, and cap), Bezier (points, segments, dash_lenght, and dash_offset,), and Mesh (mode, vertices, indices)

- The source property that applies to all the vertex instructions

- The three set of canvas instructions: canvas.before, canvas, and canvas.after

- The context instructions (and some of their properties): Color (rgba, rgb), Rotate (angle, axis,origin), Translate (x, y, xy), Scale (xyz), PushMatrix, and PopMatrix

The list is quite comprehensive, but of course there are some remaining components that we can find in the Kivy API. The important part is that we discussed the concepts behind the use of the canvas. Feel free to play with the provided examples to reinforce the important concepts of this chapter. You should feel comfortable to put things together and enliven your interface, so you can actually draw with it. The next chapter will focus on event handling and manipulating Kivy objects directly from Python.

3
Widget Events – Binding Actions

In this chapter, you will learn how to integrate actions into the **Graphical User Interface (GUI)** components; some of the actions will be associated with the canvas and others with the `Widget` management. We will learn how to handle events dynamically in order to make the application respond to the user interactions. In this chapter, you will acquire the following skills:

- Reference different parts of the GUI through IDs and properties
- Override, bind, unbind, and create Kivy events
- Add widgets to other widgets dynamically
- Add vertex and context instructions to the canvas dynamically
- Translate relative and absolute coordinates between a widget, its parent, and its window
- Use properties to keep the GUI updated with the changes

This is an exciting chapter because our application will start interacting with the user applying the concepts acquired in the previous two chapters. All the basic functionality of our *Comic Creator* project will be ready by the end. This includes shapes that can be dragged, sizeable circles, and lines, clearing the widget space, removing the last added figure, grouping several widgets to drag them together, and keeping the *status bar* updated about the last actions of the user.

Attributes, ID, and root

In *Chapter 1, GUI Basics – Building an Interface,* we distinguished between four main components for our *Comic Creator: tool box, drawing space, general options,* and *status bar.* In this chapter, we will make these components interact with each other and, therefore, we need to add some attributes to the classes of the project we created in the previous chapters. These attributes will reference different parts of the interface so that they can communicate. For example, the `ToolBox` class needs to have a reference to the `DrawingSpace` instance, so the `ToolButton` instances can draw their respective figures inside it. The following diagram shows all the relationships that are created in the `comiccreator.kv` file:

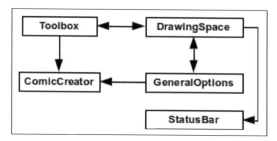

Internal References of the *Comic Creator*

We also learned in *Chapter 1, GUI Basics – Building an Interface,* that **ID** lets us reference other widgets in the Kivy language.

> The IDs are only meant to be used within the Kivy language. Therefore, we need to create attributes in order to reference the elements inside the Python code.

Following is the `comiccreator.kv` file of the *Comic Creator* project with some modifications to create the necessary IDs and attributes:

```
1.  File Name: comiccreator.kv
2.  <ComicCreator>:
3.      AnchorLayout:
4.          anchor_x: 'left'
5.          anchor_y: 'top'
6.          ToolBox:
7.              id: _tool_box
8.              drawing_space: _drawing_space
9.              comic_creator: root
```

```
10.             size_hint: None,None
11.             width: 100
12.     AnchorLayout:
13.         anchor_x: 'right'
14.         anchor_y: 'top'
15.         DrawingSpace:
16.             id: _drawing_space
17.             status_bar: _status_bar
18.             general_options: _general_options
19.             tool_box: _tool_box
20.             size_hint: None,None
21.             width: root.width - _tool_box.width
22.             height: root.height - _general_options.height -
                    _status_bar.height
23.     AnchorLayout:
24.         anchor_x: 'center'
25.         anchor_y: 'bottom'
26.         BoxLayout:
27.             orientation: 'vertical'
28.             GeneralOptions:
29.                 id: _general_options
30.                 drawing_space: _drawing_space
31.                 comic_creator: root
32.                 size_hint: 1,None
33.                 height: 48
34.             StatusBar:
35.                 id: _status_bar
36.                 size_hint: 1,None
37.                 height: 24
```

The IDs in lines 7, 16, 29, and 35 have been added to the comiccreator.kv. Following the previous diagram (Internal References of the *Comic Creator*), the IDs are used to create the attributes in lines 8, 17, 18, 19, and 30.

The names of the attributes and IDs don't have to be different. In the previous code, we just added '_' to the IDs to distinguish them from the attributes. That is to say, the _status_bar ID, is only accessible within the .kv files, and the status_bar attribute, is intended to be used inside the Python code. Both could have had the same name without causing any conflict.

As an example, line 8 created the attribute `drawing_space`, which references the `DrawingSpace` instance. This means that the `ToolBox` (line 6) instance can now access the `DrawingSpace` instance in order to draw figures on it.

One component that we often want to have access to is the base widget (`ComicCreator`) of the rule hierarchy. Lines 9 and 31 complete the referencing using **root** to have access to it through the `comic_creator` attribute.

 The reserved **root** keyword is an internal Kivy language variable that always refers to the base widget in the rule hierarchy. The other two important keywords are **self** and **app**. The keyword **self** refers to the current widget, and **app** refers to the instance of the application.

These are all the changes that are needed in the *Comic Creator* project to create the attributes. We can run the project as usual with Python `comicreator.py` and we will obtain the same result as *Chapter 2, Graphics – the Canvas*.

We created the links between the interface components with attributes. In the following sections, we will frequently use the created attributes to access different parts of the interface.

Basic widget events – dragging the stickman

Basic `Widget` events correspond to touches on the screen. However, the concept of touch in Kivy is broader than might be intuitively assumed. It includes mouse events, finger touches, and magic pen touches. For the sake of simplicity, we will often assume in this chapter that we are using a mouse but it doesn't really change if we were to use a touch screen (and the finger or magic pen instead). The following are the three basic `Widget` events:

- `on_touch_down`: When a new touch starts, for example, the action of clicking a button of the mouse or touching the screen.
- `on_touch_move`: When the touch is moved, for example, dragging the mouse or sliding the finger over the screen.
- `on_touch_up`: When the touch ends, for example, releasing the mouse button or lifting a finger from the screen.

Notice that **on_touch_down** takes place each time before **on_touch_move**, and **on_touch_up** happens; the bullet list order reflects the necessary execution order. Finally, **on_touch_move** cannot happen at all if there is no moving action. These events allow us to add drag capability to our Stickman so that we can place it wherever we want after adding it. We modify the header of comicwidgets.kv as follows:

```
38. # File name: comicwidgets.kv
39. #:import comicwidgets comicwidgets
40. <DraggableWidget>:
41.     size_hint: None, None
42.
43. <StickMan>:
44.     size: 48,48
45.     ...
```

The code now includes a rule for a new Widget called DraggableWidget. Line 41 deactivates size_hint so that we can use fixed sizes (for example, line 44). The size_hint: None, None instruction has been removed from the StickMan because it will inherit from DraggableWidget in the Python code. The **import directive** on line 39 is responsible for importing the respective comicwidgets.py file:

```
46. # File name: comicwidgets.py
47. from kivy.uix.relativelayout import RelativeLayout
48. from kivy.graphics import Line
49.
50. class DraggableWidget(RelativeLayout):
51.     def __init__(self, **kwargs):
52.         self.selected = None
53.         super(DraggableWidget, self).__init__(**kwargs)
```

The comicwidgets.py file contains the new DraggableWidget class. This class inherits from RelativeLayout (line 50). The selected attribute in line 52 will indicate whether the DraggableWidget instance is selected or not. Notice that selected is not part of Kivy; it is an attribute that we just created as part of the DraggableWidget class.

The __init__ constructor in Python is the right place to define class object attributes by simply using the self reference without declaring them at the class level; this often causes confusion to programmers coming from other object-oriented languages, such as C++ or Java.

In the comicwidgets.py file, we also have to override the three methods associated with the touch events (on_touch_down, on_touch_move, and on_touch_up). Each of these methods receives MotionEvent as a parameter (touch), which contains a lot of useful information related to the event, for instance, the coordinates of the touch, type of touch, the number of taps (or clicks), duration, the input device, and many more that can be used for advanced tasks (http://kivy.org/docs/api-kivy.input.motionevent.html#kivy.input.motionevent.MotionEvent).

Let's start with **on_touch_down**:

```
54.    def on_touch_down(self, touch):
55.        if self.collide_point(touch.x, touch.y):
56.            self.select()
57.            return True
58.        return super(DraggableWidget, self).on_touch_down(touch)
```

In line 55, we used the most common strategy in Kivy to detect if the touch is on top of a widget: the **collide_point** method. It allows us to detect whether the event actually happens inside a specific DraggableWidget by checking the coordinates of the touch.

Every active Widget receives all the touch events (MotionEvent) that happen inside the app (coordinate space), and we can use the collide_point method to detect whether the event occurs in any particular Widget.

This means it is up to the programmer to implement the logic that will discriminate between the possibility of a particular Widget doing something (in this case, to call on the method select in line 56) with the event, or whether it will just let it pass by calling the base class method (line 58) and hence, the default behavior.

The most common way of handling an event is by using `collide_point`, but other criteria can be used. Kivy gives us absolute freedom in this. Line 55 provides the simplest case of checking whether the event occurred inside the `Widget`. If the coordinate of the event was actually inside the `Widget`, we call on the `select()` method, which will set the figure as being selected (details explained later in this chapter).

It is important to understand the returning value of an event (line 57) and also what calling the method of the base class means (line 58). The Kivy GUI has a hierarchical structure, so each `Widget` instance always has a corresponding **parent** `Widget` (except if the `Widget` instance is the root of the hierarchy).

The returning value of the touch event tells the **parent** whether we took care of the event or not by returning `True` or `False`, respectively. Therefore, we need to be careful because we are in full control of the widgets that receive the event. Finally, we can also use the returning value of `super` (base class reference) to find out whether one of the children has taken care of the event already.

In general, the structure of the `on_touch_down` method overriding lines 54 to 58, is the most common way to take care of a basic event:

1. Make sure that the event happens inside `Widget` (line 55).
2. Do what has to be done (line 56).
3. Return `True` indicating that the event was processed (line 57).
4. If the event falls outside the `Widget`, then we propagate the event to the children and return the result (line 58).

Even though this is the most common way, and probably recommended for beginners, we can deviate from this in order to achieve different goals; we will soon expand this with other examples. First, let's review the `select` method:

```
59.     def select(self):
60.         if not self.selected:
61.             self.ix = self.center_x
62.             self.iy = self.center_y
63.             with self.canvas:
64.                 self.selected = Line(rectangle=
                        (0,0,self.width,self.height), dash_offset=2)
```

First, we need to ensure that nothing has been selected before (line 60) using the `select` attribute we created earlier (line 52). If this is the case, we save the center coordinates of `DraggableWidget` (lines 61 and 62), and we dynamically draw a rectangle on its border (line 63 and 64), as illustrated in the following screenshot:

Line 63 is a convenience based on the `with` Python statement. It is equivalent to the call in the **add** method with `self.canvas.add(Rectangle(...))`, with the advantage that it allows us to add many instructions at the same time. For example, we could use it to add three instructions:

```
with self.canvas:
    Color(rgb=(1,0,0))
    Line(points=(0,0,5,5))
    Rotate()
    ...
```

In *Chapter 2, Graphics – the Canvas,* we used Kivy language to add shapes to the `canvas`. Now, we used Python code directly and not the Kivy language syntax anymore, although the Python `with` statement slightly resembles it and it is frequently used in the Kivy API. Notice that we kept the `Line` instance in the `selected` attribute in line 64 because we will need it in order to remove the rectangle once the widget is not selected anymore. Also, the `DraggableWidget` instance will be aware of when it is selected, either whether it contains a reference or is `None`.

That condition is used in the `on_touch_move` method:

```
65.     def on_touch_move(self, touch):
66.         (x,y) = self.parent.to_parent(touch.x, touch.y)
67.         if self.selected and self.parent.collide_point
                (x - self.width/2, y - self.height/2):
68.             self.translate(touch.x-self.ix,touch.y-self.iy)
69.             return True
70.         return super(DraggableWidget, self).on_touch_move(touch)
```

In this event, we control the dragging of `DraggableWidget`. In line 67, we make sure that `DraggableWidget` is selected. In the same line, we use `collide_point` again but this time, we use **parent** (*drawing space*) instead of `self`. This is the reason why the previous line (line 66) transformed the widget coordinates to values that are relative to the corresponding `parent` with the **to_parent** method. In other words, we have to check the `parent` (*drawing space*) because the `Stickman` can be dragged inside the whole of the *drawing space*, and not just inside `DraggableWidget` itself. The next section will explain in detail how to localize coordinates to different parts of the screen.

Another detail of line 67 is that we check the left corner of the future position of `DraggableWidget` by subtracting half its width and height from the current touch (`touch.x - self.width/2, touch.y - self.height/2`). This is in order to make sure that we don't drag the shape outside the *drawing space* because we will drag it from the center.

If the conditions are `True`, we call the `translate` method:

```
71.     def translate(self, x, y):
72.         self.center_x = self.ix = self.ix + x
73.         self.center_y = self.iy = self.iy + y
```

The method moves the `DraggableWidget` (x, y) pixels by assigning new values to the `center_x` and `center_y` properties (lines 72 and 73). It also updates the `ix` and `iy` properties that we created in the `select` method before lines 61 and 62.

The last two lines (lines 69 and 70) of the `on_touch_move` method follow the same approach of the `on_touch_down` method (line 57 and 58), and also the `on_touch_up` method (lines 77 and 78):

```
74.     def on_touch_up(self, touch):
75.         if self.selected:
76.             self.unselect()
77.             return True
78.         return super(DraggableWidget, self).on_touch_up(touch)
```

The `on_touch_up` event undoes the `on_touch_down` status. First, it checks whether it is selected using our `selected` attribute. If it is, then it calls the `unselected()` method:

```
79.     def unselect(self):
80.         if self.selected:
81.             self.canvas.remove(self.selected)
82.             self.selected = None
```

This method will dynamically call the **remove** method to remove the `Line` vertex instruction from the `canvas` (line 81), and set our attribute `selected` to `None` (line 82) to indicate that the widget is not being dragged anymore. Notice the different ways in which we add the `Line` vertex instruction (line 63 and 64) and remove it (line 81).

There are two more lines of code in `comicwidgets.py`:

```
83. class StickMan(DraggableWidget):
84.     pass
```

These lines define our `StickMan`, which now inherits from `DraggableWidget` (line 83) instead of from `RelativeLayout`.

A final change is necessary in `drawingspace.kv`, which now looks as follows:

```
85. # File name: drawingspace.kv
86. <DrawingSpace@RelativeLayout>:
87.     Canvas.before:
88.         Line:
89.             rectangle: 0, 0, self.width - 4,self.height - 4
90.     StickMan:
```

We added a border to `canvas.before` of the *drawing space* (lines 87 and 88), which will serve us a reference to visualize where the canvas starts or ends. We also kept a `StickMan` instance in the *drawing space*. You can run the application (`python comiccreator.py`) and drag the `StickMan` over the *drawing space*.

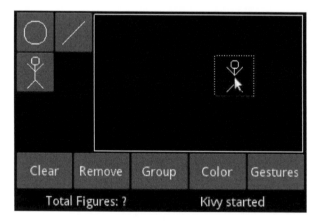

In this section, you learned the three basic touch events of any `Widget`. They are strongly dependent on the coordinates, and therefore it will be necessary to learn how to properly manipulate the coordinates. We introduce this technique in the `on_touch_move` method, but it will be the main topic in the next section, which explores the possible ways that Kivy offers to localize coordinates.

Localizing coordinates – adding stickmen

In the last section, we used the **`to_parent()`** method (line 66) to translate the coordinates relative to the `DrawingSpace`, to its parent. Remember that we were inside `DraggableWidget` and the coordinates we received were relative to `parent` (`DrawingSpace`).

These coordinates are convenient for `DraggableWidget` because we positioned it in the parent's coordinates. The method allows us to use the coordinates in the parent's `collide_point`. This is no longer convenient for when we want to check the coordinates on the parent's `parent` space or when we need to draw something directly on the canvas of a `Widget`.

Before studying more examples, let's review the theory. You learned that `RelativeLayout` is very useful because it is simpler to think inside a constraint space to localize our objects. The problems start when we need to translate coordinates to another `Widget` area. Let's consider the following screenshot of a Kivy program:

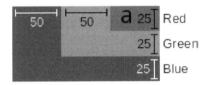

The code to generate this example is not shown here since it is very straightforward. If you want to test it, you can find the code under the folder `04 - Embedding RelativeLayouts/` and run it with `python main.py --size=150x75`. It consists of three `RelativeLayouts` embedded into each other. The **Blue** (darker gray) is parent of the **Green** (light gray) and the **Green** is parent of **Red** (middle gray). The **a** (in the top-right corner) is a `Label` instance located at the position `(5, 5)` inside **Red** (middle gray) `RelativeLayout`. The **Blue** layout (dark gray) is the size of the window (150 x 75). The rest of the elements are indicators (no part of the code) to help you understand the example.

The preceding screenshot includes some measurements that help explain the four methods of localizing coordinates that the `Widget` class provides:

- **`to_parent()`**: This method transforms relative coordinates inside `RelativeLayout` to the parent of `RelativeLayout`. For example, `red.to_parent(a.x, a.y)` returns the coordinates of a relative to the green (light gray) layout, which are `(50+5, 25+5)` = `(55, 30)`.

- **`to_local()`**: This method transforms the coordinates of `parent` of `RelativeLayout` to `RelativeLayout`. For example, `red.to_local(55,30)` returns `(5,5)`, the coordinates of a label relative to the red layout (middle gray).

- **`to_window()`**: This method transforms the coordinates of the current `Widget` to absolute coordinates with respect to the window. For example, `a.to_window(a.x, a.y)` returns the absolute coordinates of **a** which are `(100 + 5, 50 + 5)` = `(105, 55)`.

- **`to_widget()`**: This method transforms the absolute coordinates to coordinates within the parent of the current widget. For example, `a.to_widget(105,55)` returns `(5,5)`, again the coordinates of a relative to the red (middle gray) layout.

The last two methods don't use the red layout to transform the coordinates because in this case, Kivy assumes that the coordinates are always relative to the parent. There is also a `Boolean` parameter (called **relative**), which controls whether the coordinates are relative inside the `Widget`.

Let's study a real example in the *Comic Creator* project. We will add events to the *tool box* buttons, so that we can add figures to the *drawing space*. In this process, we will encounter a scenario in which we have to use one of the before-mentioned methods to localize our coordinates correctly to the `Widget`.

This code corresponds to the header of the `toolbox.py` file:

```
91.  # File name: toolbox.py
92.  import kivy
93.
94.  import math
95.  from kivy.uix.togglebutton import ToggleButton
96.  from kivy.graphics import Line
97.  from comicwidgets import StickMan, DraggableWidget
98.
99.  class ToolButton(ToggleButton):
100.    def on_touch_down(self, touch):
```

```
101.              ds = self.parent.drawing_space
102.              if self.state == 'down' and ds.collide_point
                    (touch.x, touch.y):
103.                  (x,y) = ds.to_widget(touch.x, touch.y)
104.                  self.draw(ds, x, y)
105.                  return True
106.             return super(ToolButton, self).on_touch_down(touch)
107.
108.    def draw(self, ds, x, y):
109.        pass
```

The structure in lines 99 to 106 is already familiar. Line 102 makes sure that ToolButton is in the 'down' state and that the event happened in the DrawingSpace instance (referenced by ds). Remember that the parent of ToolButton is ToolBox and that we added an attribute that references the DrawingSpace instance in comiccreator.kv at the beginning of the chapter.

The draw method is called in line 104. It will draw the respective shapes according to the derived classes (ToolStickMan, ToolCircle, and ToolLine). We need to be sure that we send the right coordinates to the draw method. Therefore, before calling it, we need to translate the absolute coordinates (received in on_touch_down of ToolButton) to relative coordinates (appropriated for the *drawing space*) with the to_widget event (line 103).

 We know that the coordinates we received (touch.x and touch.y) are absolute because ToolStickman is not RelativeLayout, whereas the DrawingSpace (ds) is.

Let's continue studying the toolbox.py file and see how ToolStickMan actually adds StickMan:

```
110. class ToolStickman(ToolButton):
111.     def draw(self, ds, x, y):
112.         sm = StickMan(width=48, height=48)
113.         sm.center = (x,y)
114.         ds.add_widget(sm)
```

We create an instance of `Stickman` (line 112), use the translated coordinates (line 103) to center the `Stickman`, and finally (line 119), add it to the `DrawingSpace` instance with the **add_widget** method (line 114). We just need to update a few lines in `toolbox.kv` in order to run the project with new changes:

```
115. # File name: toolbox.kv
116. #:import toolbox toolbox
117.
118. <ToolButton>:
119.     ...
120. <ToolBox@GridLayout>:
121.     ...
122.     ToolStickman:
```

First, we need to import `toolbox.py` (line 116), then we remove `@ToggleButton` from `ToolButton` (line 118) because we added it in `toolbox.py`, and finally we replace the last `ToolButton` for our new `ToolStickman` widget (line 122). At this point, we are able to add *stickmen* to the *drawing space* and also drag them over it.

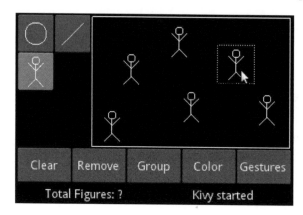

We have covered the basics now, so let's learn how to bind and unbind events dynamically.

Binding and unbinding events – sizing limbs and heads

In the previous two sections, we override basic events to perform actions we want. In this section, you will learn how to bind and unbind events dynamically. It was quite an easy job to add our Stickman because it is a Widget already, but what about the graphics, the circle, and the rectangle? We could create some widgets for them, just as we did with the Stickman, but let's attempt something braver before that. Instead of just clicking on the *drawing space*, let's drag the mouse on its border to decide the size of the circle or line:

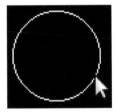

Using mouse to set the size

Once we finish the dragging (and we are satisfied with the size), let's dynamically create DraggableWidget that will contain the shape, so we can also drag them over the DrawingSpace instance. The following class diagram will help us understand the whole inheritance structure of the toolbox.py file:

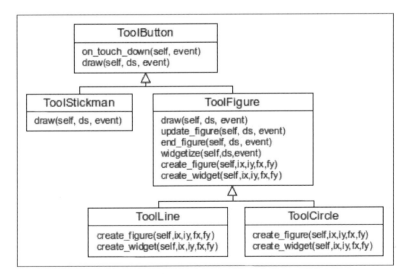

The diagram includes `ToolButton` and `ToolsStickman`, which were explained in the last section, but it also includes three new classes called `ToolFigure`, `ToolLine`, and `ToolCircle`.

The `ToolFigure` class has six methods. Let's start with a quick overview of these methods and then highlight the important and new parts:

1. draw: This method overrides `draw` of `ToolButton` (lines 108 and 109). The position where we touch down indicates the starting point of our figure, either the center for a circle or one of the ends of a line.

```
123. class ToolFigure(ToolButton):
124.     def draw(self, ds, x, y):
125.         (self.ix, self.iy) = (x,y)
126.         with ds.canvas:
127.             self.figure=self.create_figure(x,y,x+1,y+1)
128.         ds.bind(on_touch_move=self.update_figure)
129.         ds.bind(on_touch_up=self.end_figure)
```

2. update_figure: This method updates the end-point of the figure when we drag. Either the end of a line or the radius (distance from the starting point to the end point) of the circle.

```
130.     def update_figure(self, ds, touch):
131.         if ds.collide_point(touch.x, touch.y):
132.             (x,y) = ds.to_widget(touch.x, touch.y)
133.             ds.canvas.remove(self.figure)
134.             with ds.canvas:
135.                 self.figure = self.create_figure
                         (self.ix, self.iy,x,y)
```

3. end_figure: This method indicates the final end point of the figure with the same logic as in `update_figure`. Also, we put the final figure inside `DraggableWidget` (see `widgetize`).

```
136.     def end_figure(self, ds, touch):
137.         ds.unbind(on_touch_move=self.update_figure)
138.         ds.unbind(on_touch_up=self.end_figure)
139.         ds.canvas.remove(self.figure)
140.         (fx,fy) = ds.to_widget(touch.x, touch.y)
141.         self.widgetize(ds,self.ix,self.iy,fx,fy)
```

4. `widgetize`: This method creates `DraggableWidget` and places the figure in it. It uses four coordinates that have to be localized correctly with the localization methods:

```
142.     def widgetize(self,ds,ix,iy,fx,fy):
143.         widget = self.create_widget(ix,iy,fx,fy)
144.         (ix,iy) = widget.to_local(ix,iy,relative=True)
145.         (fx,fy) = widget.to_local(fx,fy,relative=True)
146.         widget.canvas.add( self.create_figure(ix,iy,fx,fy))
147.         ds.add_widget(widget)
```

5. `create_figure`: This method will be overridden by `ToolLine` (lines 153 and 154) and `ToolCircle` (lines 162 to 163). It creates the respective figure, given four coordinates:

```
148.     def create_figure(self,ix,iy,fx,fy):
149.         pass
```

6. `create_widget`: This method is also overridden by `ToolLine` (lines 156 to 159) and `ToolCircle` (lines 165 to 169). It creates a respectively positioned and sized `DraggableWidget` given four coordinates.

```
150.     def create_widget(self,ix,iy,fx,fy):
151.         pass
```

Most of the statements from the preceding methods have already been covered. The new topic of this code is the dynamic **bind/unbind** of events. The main problem we needed to solve is that we didn't want the on_touch_move and on_touch_up events active all the time. We needed to activate them (**bind**) from the moment the user starts drawing (on_touch_down of ToolButton that calls on the method draw) until the user decides the size and does a touch up. Therefore, we bound update_figure and end_figure, respectively, to the on_touch_move and on_touch_up events of DrawingSpace when the method draw is called on (lines 128 and 129). Also, we unbound them when the user ends the figure on method end_figure (lines 137 and 138). Notice that we can unbind the same method that is being executed (end_figure) from the on_touch_up event. We want to avoid calling the methods update_figure and end_figure unnecessarily. With this approach, they are going to be called only when the figure is drawn for the first time.

There are a few other interesting things in this code that deserve some attention. In line 125, we created two class attributes (self.ix and self.iy) to keep the coordinates of the initial touch. We use those coordinates each time we update the figure (line 135) and when we put the figure into a Widget (line 141).

We also use some of the localizing methods that we covered in the previous section. In lines 132 and 140, we used `to_widget` to translate the coordinates to the `DrawingSpace` instance. The lines 144 and 145 use `to_local` to translate the coordinates to `DraggableWidget`.

 DraggableWidget is instructed to translate the coordinates to its inner relative space with the parameter **relative**=True because DraggableWidget is relative and we are trying to draw inside it (not inside the parent: the *drawing space*).

There is some basic math involved in the calculation of the position and sizes of the figures and widgets. We have intentionally moved it to the deeper classes of the inheritance: `ToolLine` and `ToolCircle`. The following is their code, the last part of `toolbox.py`:

```
152. class ToolLine(ToolFigure):
153.     def create_figure(self,ix,iy,fx,fy):
154.         return Line(points=[ix, iy, fx, fy])
155.
156.     def create_widget(self,ix,iy,fx,fy):
157.         pos = (min(ix, fx), min(iy, fy))
158.         size = (abs(fx-ix), abs(fy-iy))
159.         return DraggableWidget(pos = pos, size = size)
160.
161. class ToolCircle(ToolFigure):
162.     def create_figure(self,ix,iy,fx,fy):
163.         return Line(circle=[ix,iy,math.hypot(ix-fx,iy-fy)])
164.
165.     def create_widget(self,ix,iy,fx,fy):
166.         r = math.hypot(ix-fx, iy-fy)
167.         pos = (ix-r, iy-r)
168.         size = (2*r, 2*r)
169.         return DraggableWidget(pos = pos, size = size)
```

The math involves concepts of geometry that escape the scope of this book. It is important to understand that the methods of this code section adapts the calculations to create either lines or circles. Finally, we apply some changes to the `ToolBox` class in `toolbox.kv`:

```
170. # File name: toolbox.kv
171. ...
172.
173. <ToolBox@GridLayout>:
```

```
174.      cols: 2
175.      padding: 2
176.      tool_circle: _tool_circle
177.      tool_line: _tool_line
178.      tool_stickman: _tool_stickman
179.      ToolCircle:
180.          id: _tool_circle
181.          canvas:
182.              Line:
183.                  circle: 24,24,14
184.      ToolLine:
185.          id: _tool_line
186.          canvas:
187.              Line:
188.                  points: 10,10,38,38
189.      ToolStickman:
190.          id: _tool_stickman
191.          StickMan:
192.              pos_hint: {'center_x':.5,'center_y':.5}
```

The new classes `ToolCircle` (line 179), `ToolLine` (line 184), and `ToolStickMan` (line 189) have replaced the previous `ToolButton` instances. Now, we can also add and scale lines and circles to the *drawing space*:

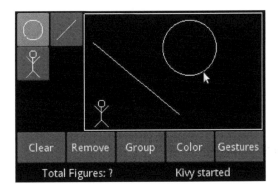

We also created some attributes (lines 176, 177, and 178) that will be useful in *Chapter 4, Improving the User Experience*, when we use gestures to create figures.

Binding events in the Kivy language

So far, we have been handling events in two ways: overridding an event method (for example, on_touch_event) and binding a personalize method to a related event method (for example, ds.bind(on_touch_move=self.update_figure)). In this section, we will discuss a different way, that is, binding events in the Kivy language. Potentially, we could have done this since the beginning of this chapter when we started working with DraggableWidget but there is a difference. If we use the Kivy language, we can easily add the event to a specific instance and not to all the instances of the same class. In this sense, it resembles dinamically binding an instance to its callback with the bind method.

We are going to concentrate on new events specific to Button and ToggleButton. The following is the code for generaloption.kv:

```
193. # File name: generaloptions.kv
194. #:import generaloptions generaloptions
195. <GeneralOptions>:
196.     orientation: 'horizontal'
197.     padding: 2
198.     Button:
199.         text: 'Clear'
200.         on_press: root.clear(*args)
201.     Button:
202.         text: 'Remove'
203.         on_release: root.remove(*args)
204.     ToggleButton:
205.         text: 'Group'
206.         on_state: root.group(*args)
207.     Button:
208.         text: 'Color'
209.         on_press: root.color(*args)
210.     ToggleButton:
211.         text: 'Gestures'
212.         on_state: root.gestures(*args)
```

The Button class has two extra events: **on_press** and **on_release**. The former is similar to on_touch_down and the latter is similar to on_touch_up. However, in this case, we don't need to worry about calling the collide_point method. We used on_press for the **Clear** Button (line 200) and the **Color** Button (line 209) and on_release for the **Remove** Button (line 203) to illustrate both methods, but for this particular case, it does not really matter which one we pick. The **on_state** event is already a part of the Button class, although more commonly used in the ToggleButton instances. This event is triggered every time the state of ToggleButton changes from 'normal' to 'down' and vice versa. The **on_state** event is used in lines 206 and 212. All the events are bound to methods in the root, which are defined in the generaloptions.py file:

```
213.  # File name: generaloptions.py
214.  from kivy.uix.boxlayout import BoxLayout
215.  from kivy.properties import NumericProperty, ListProperty
216.
217.  class GeneralOptions(BoxLayout):
218.      group_mode = False
219.      translation = ListProperty(None)
220.
221.      def clear(self, instance):
222.          self.drawing_space.clear_widgets()
223.
224.      def remove(self, instance):
225.          ds = self.drawing_space
226.          if len(ds.children) > 0:
227.              ds.remove_widget(ds.children[0])
228.
229.      def group(self, instance, value):
230.          if value == 'down':
231.              self.group_mode = True
232.          else:
233.              self.group_mode = False
234.              self.unselect_all()
235.
236.      def color(self, instance):
237.          pass
238.
239.      def gestures(self, instance, value):
240.          pass
241.
242.      def unselect_all(self):
```

```
243.            for child in self.drawing_space.children:
244.                child.unselect()
245.
246.    def on_translation(self,instance,value):
247.            for child in self.drawing_space.children:
248.                if child.selected:
249.                    child.translate(*self.translation)
```

The `GeneralOptions` method illustrates a few other methods of the `Widget` class. The `clear` method removes all the widgets from the `DrawingSpace` instance through the **clear_widgets** method (line 222). The following screenshot show the result of clicking on it:

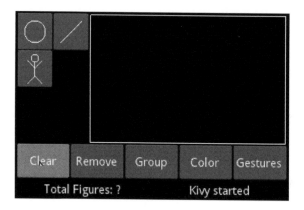

The **remove_widget** method removes the last added `Widget` instance accessing the **children** list (line 227). The `group` method modifies the `group_mode` attribute of line 218 according to the `'down'` or `'normal'` `ToggleButton` state. The `color` and `gestures` methods will be completed in *Chapter 4, Improving the User Experience*.

The *group mode* will allow the user to select several `DraggableWidget` instances in order to drag them at the same time. We activated or deactivated the *group mode* according to the state of the `ToggleButton`. In the next section, we will actually allow multiple selections and dragging in the `DraggableWidget` class. For now, we will just get the controls ready with the `unselect_all` and `on_translation` methods.

When the *group mode* is deactivated, we make sure that all the selected widgets are unselected, by calling the unselect_all method (line 242). The unselect_all method traverses the list of children calling the internal method unselect of each DraggableWidget (line 79).

Lastly, the on_translation method also traverses the children list calling the internal translate method (line 71) of each DraggableWidget. The question is; what calls the on_translation method? One of the most useful features of Kivy provides the answer to this question; this will be explained in the next section.

Creating your own events – the magical properties

This section covers the use of the Kivy properties. A Kivy property triggers an event every time we modify it. There are different types of properties, from the simple **NumericProperty** or **StringProperty** to much more complex versions such as **ListProperty**, **DictProperty**, or **ObjectProperty**. For example, if we define a **StringProperty** called text, then an on_text event is going to be triggered each time the text is modified.

> Once we define a Kivy property, Kivy internally creates an event associated with that property. The property event is referenced adding the prefix on_ to the name of the property. For example, the on_translation method (line 246) is associated with ListProperty in line 219 called translation.

All the properties work in the same way. For example, the state property that we used in the ToogleButton class is actually a property that creates the on_state event. We already used this event in line 206. We define the property and Kivy creates the event for us.

In the context of this book, a **property** will always refer to a Kivy property and it should not be confused with a Python property, which is a different concept not covered in this book. An **attribute** is used to describe variables (references, objects, and instances) that belong to the class. As a general rule, a Kivy property is always an attribute but an attribute is not necessarily a Kivy property.

In this section, we implement *group mode*, which offers the possibility of selecting and dragging several figures (DraggableWidgets instances) at the same time by pressing the **Group** button (line 204). In order to do this, we can take advantage of the relation between the translation property and the on_translation method. Basically, every time we modify the translation property, the on_translation event is triggered. Say that we drag three figures at the same time (with the *group mode*) as shown in the following screenshot:

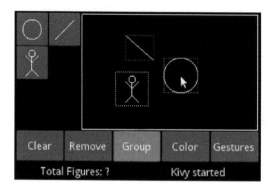

The three figures are selected but the events are handled by the circle, since it is the one that has the pointer on top. The circle needs to tell the line and the stickman to translate. Instead of calling the on_translation method, it only needs to modify the translation property, and the on_translation event is triggered. Let's include these changes in comicwidgets.py. We need four modifications.

First, we need to add the touched attribute (line 252) to indicate which of the selected figures receives the event (for example, the circle in the previous screenshot). We do this in the constructor:

```
250. def __init__(self, **kwargs):
251.     self.selected = None
252.     self.touched = False
253.     super(DraggableWidget, self).__init__(**kwargs)
```

Second, we need to set the `touched` attribute to `True` (line 256) when one of the `DraggableWidget` instances receives the event. We do this in the `on_touch_down` method:

```
254. def on_touch_down(self, touch):
255.     if self.collide_point(touch.x, touch.y):
256.         self.touched = True
257.         self.select()
258.         return True
259.     return super(DraggableWidget, self).on_touch_down(touch)
```

Third, we need to check that `DraggableWidget` is the one that is currently being touched (received the `on_touch_down` event previously). We add this to the condition in line 262. The most important change is in line 264. Instead of calling the `translate` method directly, we modify the `translation` property of *general options* (`self.parent.general_options`) setting the number of pixels the widget has been translated to the property. This will trigger the `on_translation` method of `GeneralOptions`, which at the same time calls the `translate` method for each selected `DraggableWidget`. This is the resulting code for `on_touch_move`:

```
260. def on_touch_move(self, touch):
261.     (x,y) = self.parent.to_parent(touch.x, touch.y)
262.     if self.selected and self.touched and self.parent.collide_
             point(x - self.width/2, y -self.height/2):
263.         go = self.parent.general_options
264.         go.translation=(touch.x-self.ix,touch.y-self.iy)
265.         return True
266.     return super(DraggableWidget, self).on_touch_move(touch)
```

Fourth, we need to set the `touched` attribute to `False` (line 268) on the `on_touch_up` event, and also avoid calling the `unselect` method when we use `group_mode` (line 270). Here is the code for the `on_touch_up` method:

```
267. def on_touch_up(self, touch):
268.     self.touched = False
269.     if self.selected:
270.         if not self.parent.general_options.group_mode:
271.             self.unselect()
272.     return super(DraggableWidget, self).on_touch_up(touch)
```

This example could be considered artificial, since we theoretically could have called the `on_translation` method from the start. However, properties are crucial in order to keep consistency of the internal state of a variable and the screen display. The example from the next section will improve your understanding of this.

Kivy and its properties

Even though we have only touched upon explanations of properties in the previous section, the truth is that we have been using them since the beginning of this chapter. Kivy's internals are full of properties. They are almost everywhere. For example, when we implemented `DraggableWidget`, we simply modified the `center_x` property (line 72 and 73), and the whole `Widget` was then kept updated because there is a chain of properties involved in the use of `center_x`.

The last example in this chapter illustrates how powerful Kivy properties are. Here is the code for `statusbar.py`:

```
273. # File name: statusbar.py
274. from kivy.uix.boxlayout import BoxLayout
275. from kivy.properties import NumericProperty, ObjectProperty
276.
277. class StatusBar(BoxLayout):
278.     counter = NumericProperty(0)
279.     previous_counter = 0
280.
281.     def on_counter(self, instance, value):
282.         if value == 0:
283.             self.msg_label.text="Drawing space cleared"
284.         elif value - 1 == self.__class__.previous_counter:
285.             self.msg_label.text = "Widget added"
286.         elif value + 1 == StatusBar.previous_counter:
287.             self.msg_label.text = "Widget removed"
288.         self.__class__.previous_counter = value
```

The way Kivy properties work can be perceived as confusing by some advanced Python or Java programmers. The confusion happens when a programmer assumes that `counter` (line 278) is a static attribute of the `StatusBar` class because `counter` is defined in an equivalent way to the Python static attributes (for example, `previous_counter` in line 279). The assumption is incorrect.

 Kivy properties are declared as static attribute classes (since they belong to the class), but they are always internally transformed to attribute instances. They actually belong to the object as we would have declared them in the constructor.

We need to distinguish between a static attribute of a class and an attribute of a class instance. In Python, `previous_counter` (line 279) is a static attribute of the `StatusBar` class. This means that it is shared among all the `StatusBar` instances, and it can be accessed in any of the ways shown in lines 284 and 286 (however, line 284 is recommended because it is independent of the class name). In contrast, the `selected` variable (line 251) is an attribute of a `DraggableWidget` instance. This means that there is a `selected` variable per `StatusBar` object. It is not shared among them. They are created until the constructor (`__init__`) is called. The only way to access it is through `obj.selected` (line 251). The `counter` property (line 278) behaves more similarly to the `selected` attribute than to the `previous_counter` static attribute, in the sense that there is one `counter` property and one `selected` attribute in each instance.

Now that this has been clarified, we can move on to study the example. The `counter` is defined as `NumericProperty` in line 278. It corresponds to the `on_counter` method (line 281) and modifies `Label` (`msg_text`) defined in the `statusbar.kv` file:

```
289. # File name: statusbar.kv
290. #:import statusbar statusbar
291. <StatusBar>:
292.     msg_text: _msg_label
293.     orientation: 'horizontal'
294.     Label:
295.         text: 'Total Figures: ' + str(root.counter)
296.     Label:
297.         id: _msg_label
298.         text: "Kivy started"
```

Note that we use `id` (line 297) again in order to define `msg_text` (line 292). Also, we use `counter` defined in line 278 to update the **Total Figures** message in line 295. The specific part (`str(root.counter)`) of `text` is updated automatically when `counter` is modified.

So, we just need to modify the `counter` property, and the interface is updated automatically. Let's update the counter in `drawingspace.py`:

```
299. # File name: drawingspace.py
300. from kivy.uix.relativelayout import RelativeLayout
301.
302. class DrawingSpace(RelativeLayout):
303.     def on_children(self, instance, value):
304.         self.status_bar.counter = len(self.children)
```

We updated `counter` with the length of `children` of the `DrawingSpace` in the method `on_children`. Then, `on_children` is called every time we add (line 114 or 147) or remove (line 222 or 227) widgets from the `children` list of the `DrawingSpace` because `children` is also a Kivy property.

Don't forget to import this file into `drawingspace.py` in the `drawingspace.kv` file, in which we also removed the border of the *drawing space*:

```
305. # File name: drawingspace.kv
306. #:import drawingspace drawingspace
307. <DrawingSpace@RelativeLayout>:
```

The following diagram shows a chain of elements (properties, methods, and widgets) that are associated with the `children` property:

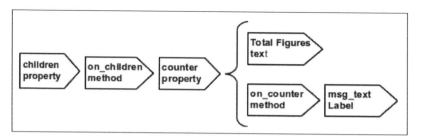

It is important to compare again the way we gain access to the `counter` property and the `msg_label` attribute. We defined the `counter` property in the `StatusBar` (line 278) and used it in `Label` through the `root` (line 295). In the `msg_label` case, we started defining `id` (line 297) and then the attribute of the Kivy language (line 292). Then, we were able used msg_label in the Python code (lines 283, 285 and 287)

Remember that an attribute is not necessarily a Kivy property. An attribute is an element of the class, whereas a Kivy property also associates the attribute with an event.

You can find the complete list of available properties in the Kivy API (http://kivy. org/docs/api-kivy.properties.html). There are two specific properties that should at least be mentioned: **BoundedNumericProperty** and **AliasProperty**. The **BoundedNumericProperty** property allows the setting of the maximum and minimum values. If the value is beyond the range, an Exception is thrown. The **AliasProperty** property offers a way in which we can extend the properties; it allows us to create our own properties in case the necessary property does not exist.

One last thing that deserves attention is that attributes of the vertex instructions are used as properties when we create them with the Kivy language. For example, if we change the position of the line inside ToolLine, it will be updated automatically. However, this just applies inside the Kivy language, not when we add the vertex instructions dynamically, as we did in toolbox.py. In our case, we had to remove and create a new vertex instruction every time we needed to update the figures (lines 133 to 135). However, we could have created our own properties to handle the updates. An example will be offered in *Chapter 6, Kivy Player – a TED Video Streamer*, when we add subtitles to the videos.

Let's run the code one last time to see the final result with the status bar counting figures and indicating our last action:

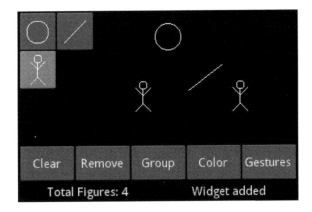

Summary

We covered most of the topics related to event handling in this chapter. You learned how to override different kind of events, dynamic binding and unbinding, assigning events in the Kivy language, and creating our own. You also learned about Kivy properties, how to manage the localization of coordinates to different widgets, and many methods related to adding, removing, and updating objects of Kivy `Widget` and `canvas`. Here are the events, methods, properties, and attributes that were covered:

- The events we covered are `on_touch_up`, `on_touch_move` and `on_touch_down` (of `Widget`); `on_press` and `on_release` (of `Button`); and `on_state` (of `ToggleButton`)

- The attributes we covered are x and y of `MotionEvent` (touch); `center_x`, `center_y`, `canvas`, `parent`, and `children` of `Widget`, and `state` of `ToggleButton`.

- The following methods of `Widget`:
  - `bind` and `unbind` to attach events dynamically
  - `collide_points`, `to_parent`, `to_local`, `to_window`, and `to_widget` to work with coordinates
  - `add_widget`, `remove_widget`, and `clear_widgets` to dynamically modify the children widgets
  - The methods `add` and `remove` of canvas to dynamically add and remove vertex and context instructions

- Kivy properties: `NumericProperty` and `ListProperty`

There are two other important types of events related to the clock and keyboard. This chapter was focused on widget and property events but we will see how to use other events in *Chapter 5, Invaders Revenge – an Interactive Multi-touch Game*. The next chapter is going to introduce a list of interesting topics on Kivy in order to improve the user experience with our *Comic Creator*.

4
Improving the User Experience

This chapter presents an overview of useful components that Kivy provides to make the programmer's life easier when it is time to improve the user experience. Some Kivy components reviewed in this chapter are related to widgets that include very particular functionalities (for example, a color palette); in this case, you will learn the basic techniques to control them. Other widgets will help us expand the use of the canvas, for example, changing the color, rotating and scaling shapes, or handling gestures. Finally, we will quickly improve the look and feel of the application with a few tips. All the sections are intended to increase the usability of the application and are self-contained. The following is the list of topics we will review in the chapter:

- Switching between different screens
- Using the Kivy palette widget to select colors
- Controlling the visible area of the canvas
- Rotating and scaling with multi-touch gestures
- Creating single gestures to draw on the screen
- Enhancing the design with a few global changes

More importantly, we will discuss how to incorporate these topics into a current working project. This will reinforce your previously acquired knowledge and explore a new programming situation in which we need to add functionality to an existent code. At the end of this chapter, you should feel comfortable with exploring all the different widgets that the Kivy API offers, and quickly understand how to integrate them into your code.

ScreenManager – selecting colors for the figures

The **ScreenManager** class lets us handle different screens in the same window. In Kivy, screens are preferred over windows, because we are programming for different devices with different screen sizes. Therefore, it is difficult (if not impossible) to have windows that adapt properly to all devices. Just imagine yourself juggling windows with your fingers on your mobile phone.

So far, all our figures have been of the same color. Let's allow the user to add some color to make the *Comic Creator* more versatile. Kivy provides us with a `Widget` called **ColorPicker**, which is displayed in the following screenshot:

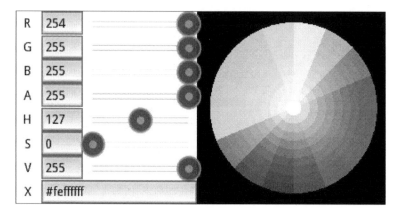

As you can see, this `Widget` requires a wide space, so it would be difficult to accommodate it in our current interface.

> There is a bug in Kivy 1.9.0 that prevents `ColorPicker` from working in Python 3 (it is already fixed in the development version 1.9.1-dev, which is available at `https://github.com/kivy/kivy/`). You can use Python 2, or there is an alternative code for Python 3 included in the code that you can download from the Packt Publishing website. Instead of the `ColorPicker`, there is a widget based on `GridLayout` to select a few colors. The concepts that we will discuss in this section are also reflected in that code.

The **ScreenManager** class allows us to have multiple screens instead of just one `Widget` (`ComicCreator`), and also lets us switch easily between the screens. Here is a new Kivy file (`comicscreenmanager.kv`) that contains the `ComicScreenManager` class definition:

```
1.  # File name: comicscreenmanager.kv
2.  #:import FadeTransition kivy.uix.screenmanager.FadeTransition
3.  <ComicScreenManager>:
4.      transition: FadeTransition()
5.      color_picker: _color_picker
6.      ComicCreator:
7.      Screen:
8.          name: 'colorscreen'
9.          ColorPicker:
10.             id: _color_picker
11.             color: 0,.3,.6,1
12.             Button:
13.                 text: "Select"
14.                 pos_hint: {'center_x': .75, 'y': .05}
15.                 size_hint: None, None
16.                 size: 150, 50
17.                 on_press: root.current = 'comicscreen'
```

We embedded the `ColorPicker` instance inside a **Screen** widget (line 7), instead of adding it directly to the `ComicScreenManager`.

 A **ScreenManager** instance must contain widgets of the **Screen** base class. No other types of `Widget` (label, button, or layouts) are allowed.

Since we have also added our `ComicCreator` to `ScreenManager` (line 6), we need to make sure that our `ComicCreator` inherits from the `Screen` class in the `comiccreator.kv` file, so we need to change the file header:

```
18. # File name: comiccreator.kv
19. <ComicCreator@Screen>:
20.     name: 'comicscreen'
21.     AnchorLayout:…
```

The **name** property (line 20) is used to identify the screen with an ID, in this case comicscreen, and it is used to change between the screens of ScreenManeger through its **current** property. For example, the Button instance that we added to ColorPicker (line 12), uses the name property to change the current screen in the on_press event (line 17). The root refers to the ScreenManager class and the **current** property tells it what the active Screen is. In this case comicscreen, the name we assigned to identify the ComicCreator instance. Notice that we add the Python code directly (line 17) instead of calling a method as we did in *Chapter 3, Widget Events – Binding Actions.*

We also gave a name (colorscreen) to the screen that contains the ColorPicker instance. We will use this name to activate ColorPicker with the **Color** button in the *general options* area. We need to modify the color method of generaloptions.py:

```
22. def color(self, instance):
23.     self.comic_creator.manager.current = 'colorscreen'
```

The **Color** button now switches the screen in order to display the ColorPicker instance. Notice the way we access ScreenManager (line 23). First, we use the comic_creator reference in the GeneralOptions class to access the ComicCreator instance. Second, we use the **manager** attribute of Screen to access its corresponding ScreenManager. Finally, we change current Screen, analogous to line 17.

ComicScreenManager now becomes the main Widget of the ComicCreator project so the comicreator.py file has to change accordingly:

```
24. # File name: comiccreator.py
25. from kivy.app import App
26. from kivy.lang import Builder
27. from kivy.uix.screenmanager import ScreenManager
28.
29. Builder.load_file('toolbox.kv')
30. Builder.load_file('comicwidgets.kv')
31. Builder.load_file('drawingspace.kv')
32. Builder.load_file('generaloptions.kv')
33. Builder.load_file('statusbar.kv')
34. Builder.load_file('comiccreator.kv')
35.
36. class ComicScreenManager(ScreenManager):
37.     pass
38.
39. class ComicScreenManagerApp(App):
```

```
40.      def build(self):
41.          return ComicScreenManager()
42.
43. if __name__=="__main__":
44.      ComicScreenManagerApp().run()
```

Since we changed the name of the app to ComicScreenManagerApp (line 44), we explicitly load the comiccreator.kv file (line 34). Remember that the comicscreenmanager.kv file is going to be called automatically since the name of the app is now ComicScreenManagerApp.

One last interesting thing about the ScreenManager is that we can use **transitions**. Just as an example, the lines 2 and 4 import and use a simple **FadeTransition**.

> Kivy provides a set of transitions (**FadeTransition**, **SwapTransition**, **SlideTransition**, and **WipeTransition**) to switch between the Screen instances of ScreenManager. Check the Kivy API for more information on how to customize them with different parameters at http://kivy.org/docs/api-kivy.uix.screenmanager.html

After these changes, we can switch between the two screens, ColorPicker and ComicCreator, by clicking on the Color button of *general options*, or the Select button of ColorPicker. We also set a different color in the ColorPicker instance with the **color** property (line 11); however, the selection of the color still has no effect on the drawing process. The next section covers how to set the selected color to the figures we draw.

Color control on the canvas – coloring figures

The previous section focused on the selection of colors from a canvas but this selection didn't really have an effect yet. In this section, we will actually use the selected color. Assigning a color can be tricky if we are not careful. If you recall, in *Chapter 3, Widget Events – Binding Actions*, Color is a context instruction that we must add to the canvas. Moreover, we have to be sure that we add the instruction before we draw the actual figure. Basically, selecting a color is similar to picking a crayon color to draw on a piece of paper. Until you change the crayon, you will continue drawing with its color.

When the color of the context changes, it stays in that state until some other instruction modifies it explicitly. In *Chapter 2, Graphics – the Canvas*, we use PushMatrix and PopMatrix for a similar problem but they only apply to transformation instructions (Translate, Rotate, and Scale) because they relate to the coordinate space (that explains the matrix part of the instructions names: PushMatrix and PopMatrix).

Let's study a small example (from the *Comic Creator* project) to understand this concept better:

```
45. # File name: color.py
46. from kivy.app import App
47. from kivy.uix.gridlayout import GridLayout
48. from kivy.lang import Builder
49.
50. Builder.load_string("""
51. <GridLayout>:
52.     cols:2
53.     Label:
54.         color: 0.5,0.5,0.5,1
55.         canvas:
56.             Rectangle:
57.                 pos: self.x + 10, self.y + 10
58.                 size: self.width - 20, self.height - 20
59.     Widget:
60.         canvas:
61.             Rectangle:
62.                 pos: self.x + 10, self.y + 10
63.                 size: self.width - 20, self.height - 20
64. """)
65.
66. class LabelApp(App):
67.     def build(self):
68.         return GridLayout()
69.
70. if __name__=="__main__":
71.     LabelApp().run()
```

Notice that we use the **load_string** method of the **Builder** class instead of using the **load_file** method. This method allows us to embed Kivy language statements inside a Python code file.

One of the properties of Label is called color; it changes the color of the Label text. We change color to gray (line 54) in the first Label but it doesn't clean the context. Observe the result in the following screenshot:

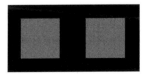

The rectangle of Label (line 56), but also the rectangle of Widget (Line 61) have both changed color. Kivy tries to keep all its components as simple as possible to avoid unnecessary instructions. We will follow this approach for the colors, so we won't worry about the color until we need to use it. Any other components can take care of their own color.

We can now implement the changes in the *Comic Creator*. There are only three methods where we draw in the *drawing space* (all of them are in the toolbox.py file). Here are those methods with the corresponding new lines highlighted:

- The draw method in the ToolStickman class:

```
72. def draw(self, ds, x, y):
73.     sm = StickMan(width=48, height=48)
74.     sm.center = (x,y)
75.     screen_manager = self.parent.comic_creator.manager
76.     color_picker = screen_manager.color_picker
77.     sm.canvas.before.add(Color(*color_picker.color))
78.     ds.add_widget(sm)
```

- The draw method in the ToolFigure class:

```
79. def draw(self, ds, x, y):
80.     (self.ix, self.iy) = (x,y)
81.     screen_manager = self.parent.comic_creator.manager
82.     color_picker = screen_manager.color_picker
83.     with ds.canvas:
84.         Color(*color_picker.color)
85.         self.figure=self.create_figure(x,y,x+1,y+1)
86.     ds.bind(on_touch_move=self.update_figure)
87.     ds.bind(on_touch_up=self.end_figure)
```

- The `widgetize` method in the `ToolFigure` class:

```
88. def widgetize(self,ds,ix,iy,fx,fy):
89.     widget = self.create_widget(ix,iy,fx,fy)
90.     (ix,iy) = widget.to_local(ix,iy,relative=True)
91.     (fx,fy) = widget.to_local(fx,fy,relative=True)
92.     screen_manager = self.parent.comic_creator.manager
93.     color_picker = screen_manager.color_picker
94.     widget.canvas.add(Color(*color_picker.color))
95.     widget.canvas.add(self.create_figure(ix,iy,fx,fy))
96.     ds.add_widget(widget)
```

All three methods have a pair of specific instructions in common; you can find them in lines 75 and 76, 81 and 82, and 92 and 93. These are reference chains to get access to the `ColorPicker` instance. After this, we just add a `Color` instruction to the canvas (as we learned in *Chapter 2, Graphics – the Canvas*) using the selected `color` in `color_picker` (lines 77, 84, and 94).

 The "splat" operator (*) on lines 77, 84, and 94 is used in Python to unpack argument lists. In this case, the `Color` constructor is meant to receive three parameters with the red, green, and blue values, but we have a list stored in `color_picker.color`, for example, (1, 0, 1), so we need to unpack it to get three separated values 1, 0, 1.

We also use `canvas.before` in the `draw` method of the `ToolStickman` class (line 77). This is used to ensure that the `Color` instruction is executed before the instructions we added in `canvas` of `Stickman` (the `comicwidgets.kv` file). This is not necessary in the other two methods because we have full control of the canvas order inside those methods.

Finally, we must import the `Color` class in the header of the file `from kivy.graphics import Line, Color`. We can now take a break and enjoy the result of our hard work with our *Comic Creator*:

At a later point in time, we can discuss whether our drawing is just an avid *Comic Creator* fan or a narcissistic alien with an oversized t-shirt. For now, it seems more useful to learn how to limit the *drawing space* to the specific area that occupies the window.

StencilView – limiting the drawing space

In *Chapter 3*, *Widget Events – Binding Actions*, we avoided drawing outside of the *drawing space* by using simple mathematics and `collide_points`. It was far from perfect (for example, it fails in the group mode or when we resize it), and it was tedious and prone to programming mistakes.

That was sufficient for a first example, however, **StencilView** is the easier way to go here. **StencilView** limits the drawing area to the space occupied by itself. Anything drawn outside that area is hidden. First, let's modify the file drawingspace.py with the following header:

```
97.  # File name: drawingspace.py
98.  from kivy.uix.stencilview import StencilView
99.
100. class DrawingSpace(StencilView):
101.     ...
```

The DrawingSpace instance inherits now from StencilView, instead of RelativeLayout. The StencilView class doesn't use relative coordinates (as the RelativeLayout class does) but we would like to keep relative coordinates in the *drawing space* because they are convenient for drawing purposes. In order to do this, we can modify the top-right AnchorLayout, so the DrawingSpace instance is inside a RelativeLayout instance. We do this in the comiccreator.kv file:

```
102.     AnchorLayout:
103.         anchor_x: 'right'
104.         anchor_y: 'top'
105.         RelativeLayout:
106.             size_hint: None,None
107.             width: root.width - _tool_box.width
108.             height: root.height - _general_options.height -
                 _status_bar.height
109.             DrawingSpace:
110.                 id: _drawing_space
111.                 general_options: _general_options
112.                 tool_box: _tool_box
113.                 status_bar: _status_bar
```

When we embed the DrawingSpace instance (line 109) inside a RelativeLayout instance (line 105) of the same size (by default, the DrawingSpace instance uses size_hint: 1, 1 occupying all the area of the RelativeLayout parent), then the coordinates inside the DrawingSpace instance are relative to the RelativeLayout instance. Since they are of the same size, then the coordinates are also relative to the DrawingSpace instance.

We kept the DrawingSpace ID (line 110) and attributes (lines 111 to 113). Since we have a new level of indentation and the DrawingSpace class is not relative itself, this affects the way we localize the coordinates in the ToolBox instance, specifically, in on_touch_down of the ToolButton class, and update_figure and end_figure of the ToolFigure class. The following is the new code for on_touch_down of the ToolButton class:

```
114.        def on_touch_down(self, touch):
115.            ds = self.parent.drawing_space
116.            if self.state == 'down' and\
                    ds.parent.collide_point(touch.x, touch.y):
117.                (x,y) = ds.to_widget(touch.x, touch.y)
118.                self.draw(ds, x, y)
119.                return True
120.            return super(ToolButton,
                    self).on_touch_down(touch)
```

We receive absolute coordinates in this method since we are inside ToolButton, which doesn't belong to any RelativeLayout instance. The *drawing space* also receives absolute coordinates, but it will interpret them inside the context of the RelativeLayout instance that it is embedded in. The right approach for the DrawingSpace instance is to ask its RelativeLayout parent who will collide the coordinates (received in the ToolButton) correctly (line 116)

The following is the new code of update_figure and end_figure of the ToolFigure class:

```
121. def update_figure(self, ds, touch):
122.     ds.canvas.remove(self.figure)
123.     with ds.canvas:
124.         self.figure = self.create_figure(self.ix,
                 self.iy,touch.x,touch.y)
125.
126. def end_figure(self, ds, touch):
127.     ds.unbind(on_touch_move=self.update_figure)
128.     ds.unbind(on_touch_up=self.end_figure)
129.     ds.canvas.remove(self.figure)
130.     self.widgetize(ds,self.ix,self.iy,touch.x,touch.y)
```

We removed some instructions because we no longer need them. First off, we don't need to use the `to_widget` method anymore in either of the two methods, since we are already getting the coordinates from the `RelativeLayout` parent. And secondly, we don't need to worry about applying the `collide_point` method in the `update_figure` method because `StencilView` will be in charge of it; any drawing that takes place outside the bounds is discarded.

With just a few changes, we ensured that nothing will be drawn outside of the *drawing space*, and, with that guarantee, we can now proceed to discuss how to drag, rotate, and scale the figures.

Scatter – multi-touching to drag, rotate, and scale

In the previous chapter (*Chapter 3, Widget Events – Binding Actions*), you learned how to use events to drag widgets. You learned how to use the `on_touch_up`, `on_touch_move`, and `on_touch_down` events. However, the **Scatter** class already provides that functionality and also lets us scale and rotate using two fingers, as one would on a mobile or tablet screen. All the functionality is included inside the **Scatter** class; however, we need to apply a few changes to keep our project consistent. In particular, we still want our *group mode* to work, so that translating, scaling, and rotating can happen at the same time. Let us implement the changes in four big steps in the `comicwidgets.py` file:

1. Replace the `DraggableWidget` base class. Let's use `Scatter` instead of `RelativeLayout` (line `132` and `135`):

    ```
    131. # File name: comicwidgets.py
    132. from kivy.uix.scatter import Scatter
    133. from kivy.graphics import Line
    134.
    135. class DraggableWidget(Scatter):
    ```

 Both `Scatter` and `RelativeLayout` use relative coordinates.

2. Make sure that the on_touch_down event of DraggableWidget is sent to the base class (Scatter) by calling the super method (line 140) before return True (line 141) inside the condition. If you don't do that, the Scatter base class will never receive the event on_touch_down and nothing will happen:

```
136. def on_touch_down(self, touch):
137.     if self.collide_point(touch.x, touch.y):
138.         self.touched = True
139.         self.select()
140.         super(DraggableWidget,
                 self).on_touch_down(touch)
141.         return True
142.     return super(DraggableWidget,
             self).on_touch_down(touch)
```

 The super method is useful for the base class (Scatter) and the return statement is useful for the parent (DrawingSpace)

3. Remove the on_touch_move method and add an on_pos method, which is called when the pos property is modified. Since Scatter will be responsible for dragging, we don't need on_touch_move anymore. Instead, we will use the pos property that is modified by Scatter. Remember that the properties trigger an event that will call on the on_pos method:

```
143. def on_pos(self, instance, value):
144.     if self.selected and self.touched:
145.         go = self.parent.general_options
146.         go.translation = (self.center_x- self.ix,
                 self.center_y - self.iy)
147.         self.ix = self.center_x
148.         self.iy = self.center_y
```

4. Scatter has two other properties: rotation and scale. We can use the same idea as with pos and on_pos, and add the on_rotation and on_scale methods:

```
149.     def on_rotation(self, instance, value):
150.         if self.selected and self.touched:
151.             go = self.parent.general_options
152.             go.rotation = value
153.
154.     def on_scale(self, instance, value):
155.         if self.selected and self.touched:
156.             go = self.parent.general_options
157.             go.scale = value
```

The on_rotation and on_scale methods modify a couple of new properties (lines 152 and 157) that we need to add to the GeneralOptions class. This will help us to keep the group mode working. The following code is the new header of generaloptions.py that includes the new properties:

```
158. # File name: generaloptions.py
159. from kivy.uix.boxlayout import BoxLayout
160. from kivy.properties import NumericProperty, ListProperty
161.
162. class GeneralOptions(BoxLayout):
163.     group_mode = False
164.     translation = ListProperty(None)
165.     rotation = NumericProperty(0)
166.     scale = NumericProperty(0)
```

We import NumericProperty along with ListProperty (line 160); and we create the two missing properties: rotation and scale (lines 165 and 166). We also need to add the on_rotation (line 167) and on_scale (line 172) methods (associated with the rotation and scale properties), which will ensure that all the selected components are rotated or scaled at once, by traversing the list of children that have been added to the *drawing space* (line 173 and 177):

```
167     def on_rotation(self, instance, value):
168.         for child in self.drawing_space.children:
169.             if child.selected and not child.touched:
170.                 child.rotation = value
171.
172.     def on_scale(self, instance, value):
173.         for child in self.drawing_space.children:
174.             if child.selected and not child.touched:
175.                 child.scale = value
```

A final modification is necessary. We need to change the on_translation method to check that the current child in the loop is not the one being touched (if this happens, call the police!), because this could cause an infinitive recursion since we modify the properties that call on this event in the first place. Here is the new on_translation method in the generaloptions.py file:

```
176.     def on_translation(self,instance,value):
177.         for child in self.drawing_space.children:
178.             if child.selected and not child.touched:
179.                 child.translate(*self.translation)
```

At this point, we are able to translate, rotate, or scale the figures with our fingers, even in the *group mode*.

 Kivy provides a way to simulate multi-touch with the mouse. It is limited but you can still test this section with your one-mouse laptop. All you have to do is right-click on the figure you want to rotate. A translucent red circle will appear on the screen. Then, you can use the normal left dragging as if it were a second finger to rotate or scale. To clear the simulated multi-touch, you left-click on the red icon.

The next screenshot cut shows our StickMan being rotated and scaled at the same time as the line next to him. The small StickMan on the right is just a reference to compare against the original size. The simulated multi-touch gesture is being applied to the line on the right and that is why you can see a red (gray in the printed version) dot:

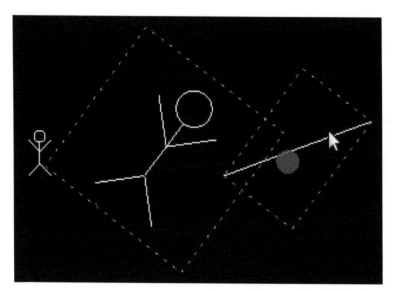

In *Chapter 1, GUI Basics – Building an Interface*, we briefly mention **ScatterLayout** but now the difference between **ScatterLayout** and **Scatter** may be clear.

ScatterLayout is a Kivy layout that inherits from `Scatter` and contains `FloatLayout`. This allows you to use the `size_hint` and `pos_hint` properties when you add widgets inside it. `ScatterLayout` also uses relative coordinates. This doesn't mean you cannot add other widgets inside a simple `Scatter`; it just means that `Scatter` doesn't honor `size_hint` or `pos_hint`.

With the use of `Scatter`, we are able to drag, rotate, and scale our figures. This is a great improvement of functionality in our *Comic Creator*. Let's now increase the interaction with the user even more, learn how to create our own gestures, and use them inside our project.

Recording gestures – line, circle, and cross

What about drawing with one finger? Can we recognize gestures? It is possible to do this with Kivy. First, we need to record the gestures that we want to use. A gesture is represented as a long string that contains the points of a stroke over the screen. The following code uses the Kivy `Gesture` and `GestureDatabase` classes to record gesture strokes. It can be run with Python `gesturerecorder.py`:

```
180. # File Name: gesturerecorder.py
181. from kivy.app import App
182. from kivy.uix.floatlayout import FloatLayout
183. from kivy.graphics import Line, Ellipse
184. from kivy.gesture import Gesture, GestureDatabase
185.
186. class GestureRecorder(FloatLayout):
187.
188.     def on_touch_down(self, touch):
189.         self.points = [touch.pos]
190.         with self.canvas:
191.             Ellipse(pos=(touch.x-5,touch.y-5),size=(10,10))
192.             self.Line = Line(points=(touch.x, touch.y))
193.
194.     def on_touch_move(self, touch):
195.         self.points += [touch.pos]
196.         self.line.points += [touch.x, touch.y]
197.
198.     def on_touch_up(self, touch):
```

```
199.            self.points += [touch.pos]
200.            gesture = Gesture()
201.            gesture.add_stroke(self.points)
202.            gesture.normalize()
203.            gdb = GestureDatabase()
204.            print ("Gesture:",
                gdb.gesture_to_str(gesture).decode(encoding='UTF-8'))
205.
206. class GestureRecorderApp(App):
207.      def build(self):
208.            return GestureRecorder()
209.
210. if __name__=="__main__":
211.      GestureRecorderApp().run()
```

The previous code prints the gesture string representations using the **Gesture** and **GestureDatabase** classes (line 184). The on_touch_down, on_touch_move, and on_touch_up methods collect points of the stroke lines 189, 195, and 199. The following screenshots are examples of strokes collected with gesturerecorded.py:

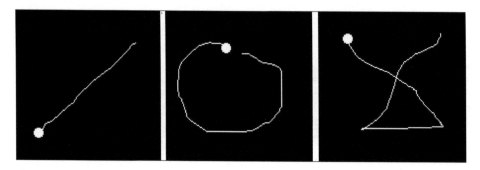

The small Circle in the preceding figures (lines 190 and 191) indicates the starting point, and the line indicates the path that the stroke follows. The most relevant part is coded in lines 200 to 204. We create Gesture (line 200), add points for the stroke with the **add_stroke** method (line 201), **normalize** to a default number of points (line 202), and create a GestureDatabase instance (line 203) that we use in line 204 to generate the string (**gesture_to_str**) and print it on the screen.

The following screenshot shows the terminal output for the stroke line (corresponding to the first figure on the left in the preceding figures set):

```
[DEBUG  ] [Base       ] Create provider from mouse
[INFO   ] [Base       ] Start application main loop
Gesture: eNq1VktuI0cM3fdFrM0I/LN4AWUbwAcI/BFsYwa2IGmSmduHxZa77bGTziKtjQ3W42MXH4v
k5unr058/tw/70/n7cT/8dvl7gGFzf8Dh+up0Pr583Z+uhgMNm28HHjafelwXbDhI99P0O7w8PZ+7m3U
3/we33ztqOLTuFen1Mx0Qht0X2KowMIZ7C2zkbThdX/3ox1jHEtpUHN3JAE2G0+3Nv8ZAqivx8PAaAEJ
```

In the preceding screenshot, the long string starting with `'eNq1Vktu...'` is the gesture serialization. We use these long strings as descriptors of the gestures that Kivy understands and uses to associate the stroke with any action we want to perform. The next section explains how to achieve this.

Recognizing gestures – drawing with the finger

The previous section explained how to obtain string representations from gestures. The current section explains how to use those string representations to recognize the gestures. Kivy has some tolerance error in the gesture recognition, so you don't have to worry about repeating exactly the same stroke.

To start, we copied the strings that were generated from the strokes in the previous section into a new file called gestures.py. The strings are assigned to different variables. The following code corresponds to gestures.py:

```
212. # File Name: gestures.py
213. line45_str = 'eNq1VktuI0cM3fdFrM0I...
214. circle_str = 'eNq1WMtuGzkQvM+P2JcI/Sb5A9rrA...
215. cross_str = 'eNq1V9tuIzcMfZ8fSV5qiH...
```

Only the first few characters of the strings are shown in the previous code but you can download the complete file from the Packt Publishing website, or use the previous section to generate your own strings.

Next, we will use these strings in the `drawingspace.py` file. Let's start importing the necessary classes in the header first:

```
216. # File name: drawingspace.py
217. from kivy.uix.stencilview import StencilView
218. from kivy.gesture import Gesture, GestureDatabase
219. from gestures import line45_str, circle_str, cross_str
220.
221. class DrawingSpace(StencilView):
```

In the preceding code, we import the `Gesture` and `GestureDatabase` classes (line 218) along with the gesture string representations added to `gestures.py` (lines 219). We added several methods to the `DrawingSpace` class. Let's quickly review each of the methods, and, at the end, highlight the key parts:

- `__init__`: This method creates the attributes of the class and fills `GestureDatabase` using **str_to_gesture** in order to transform the strings into gestures, and **add_gesture** to add the gestures to the database:

```
222. def __init__(self, *args, **kwargs):
223.     super(DrawingSpace, self).__init__()
224.     self.gdb = GestureDatabase()
225.     self.line45 = self.gdb.str_to_gesture(line45_str)
226.     self.circle = self.gdb.str_to_gesture(circle_str)
227.     self.cross = self.gdb.str_to_gesture(cross_str)
228.     self.line135 = self.line45.rotate(90)
229.     self.line225 = self.line45.rotate(180)
230.     self.line315 = self.line45.rotate(270)
231.     self.gdb.add_gesture(self.line45)
232.     self.gdb.add_gesture(self.line135)
233.     self.gdb.add_gesture(self.line225)
234.     self.gdb.add_gesture(self.line315)
235.     self.gdb.add_gesture(self.circle)
236.     self.gdb.add_gesture(self.cross)
```

- `activate` and `deactivate`: These methods bind or unbind the methods to the touch events in order to start the gesture recognition mode. These methods are called by the gesture `Button` of the *general options*:

```
237. def activate(self):
238.     self.tool_box.disabled = True
239.     self.bind(on_touch_down=self.down,
240.               on_touch_move=self.move,
```

```
241.                     on_touch_up=self.up)
242.
243. def deactivate(self):
244.      self.unbind(on_touch_down=self.down,
245.                  on_touch_move=self.move,
246.                  on_touch_up=self.up)
247.      self.tool_box.disabled = False
```

- down, move and ups: These methods record the points of the stroke in a very similar way that the previous section did:

```
248. def down(self, ds, touch):
249.     if self.collide_point(*touch.pos):
250.         self.points = [touch.pos]
251.         self.ix = self.fx = touch.x
252.         self.iy = self.fy = touch.y
253.     return True
254.
255. def move(self, ds, touch):
256.     if self.collide_point(*touch.pos):
257.         self.points += [touch.pos]
258.         self.min_and_max(touch.x, touch.y)
259.     return True
260.
261. def up(self, ds, touch):
262.     if self.collide_point(*touch.pos):
263.         self.points += [touch.pos]
264.         self.min_and_max(touch.x, touch.y)
265.         gesture = self.gesturize()
266.         recognized = self.gdb.find(gesture,
                 minscore=0.50)
267.         if recognized:
268.             self.discriminate(recognized)
269.     return True
```

- gesturize: This method creates a Gesture instance from the collected points in the previous methods:

```
270. def gesturize(self):
271.     gesture = Gesture()
272.     gesture.add_stroke(self.points)
273.     gesture.normalize()
274.     return gesture
```

- min_and_max: This method keeps track of the extreme points of the stroke:

```
275. def min_and_max(self, x, y):
276.      self.ix = min(self.ix, x)
277.      self.iy = min(self.iy, y)
278.      self.fx = max(self.fx, x)
279.      self.fy = max(self.fy, y)
```

- Discriminate: This method calls the corresponding method according to the recognized gesture:

```
280. def discriminate(self, recognized):
281.      if recognized[1] == self.cross:
282.          self.add_stickman()
283.      if recognized[1] == self.circle:
284.          self.add_circle()
285.      if recognized[1] == self.line45:
286.          self.add_line(self.ix,self.iy,self.fx,self.fy)
287.      if recognized[1] == self.line135:
288.          self.add_line(self.ix,self.fy,self.fx,self.iy)
289.      if recognized[1] == self.line225:
290.          self.add_line(self.fx,self.fy,self.ix,self.iy)
291.      if recognized[1] == self.line315:
292.          self.add_line(self.fx,self.iy,self.ix,self.fy)
```

- add_circle, add_Line, add_stickman: These methods use the corresponding ToolButton of ToolBox to add a figure according to the recognized gesture:

```
293. def add_circle(self):
294.      cx = (self.ix + self.fx)/2.0
295.      cy = (self.iy + self.fy)/2.0
296.      self.tool_box.tool_circle.widgetize(self, cx, cy,
              self .fx, self.fy)
297.
298. def add_line(self,ix,iy,fx,fy):
299.      self.tool_box.tool_line.widgetize(self,ix,iy,fx,fy)
300.
301. def add_stickman(self):
302.      cx = (self.ix + self.fx)/2.0
303.      cy = (self.iy + self.fy)/2.0
304.      self.tool_box.tool_stickman.draw(self,cx,cy)
```

- `on_children`: This method keeps the counter of the *Status Bar* updated:

```
305. def on_children(self, instance, value):
306.     self.status_bar.counter = len(self.children)
```

The `DrawingSpace` class is now in charge of capturing strokes on the screen, search for them in the gesture database (that contains the gestures of the last section), and draw a shape accordingly. It also offers the possibility of activating and deactivating the gesture recognition. Let's cover this in four parts.

First, we need to create the `GestureDatabase` instance (line 224) and use it to create the gestures from the strings (lines 225 to 227). We rotate the `line45` gesture by 90 degrees (lines 228 to 230) four times with the **rotate** method, so the `GestureDatabase` instance recognizes the line gesture in different directions. Then, we load `GestureDatabase` with the generated gestures (lines 231 to 236). We added all of these instructions in the constructor of the class, the __init__ method (lines 222 to 236), so the `DrawingSpace` class has all the elements to recognize gestures.

Second, we need to capture the gesture stroke. In order to do this, we use the touch events. We have created the methods associated with them: down (line 248), move (line 255), and up (line 261). These methods are similar to the `on_touch_down`, `on_touch_move`, and `on_touch_up` methods of the last section in the sense that they register the points of the stroke. However, they also keep track of the *extreme* axes of the stroke to define a bounding box for the stroke as the following figure illustrates:

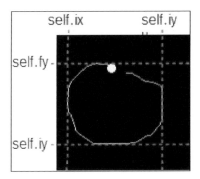

These points are used to define the size of the shape we will draw. The up method, firstly, uses the registered points to create a `Gesture` instance (line 265), secondly, makes the query to the `GestureDatabase` instance using the **find** method (line 266), and thirdly, calls the `discriminate` method to draw the appropriate shape (line 280). The **minscore** parameter of the **find** method (line 266) is used to indicate the precision of the search.

We use a low level (0.50) since we know that the strokes are very different, and that a mistake in this application can be easily undone.

Third, we implement the `discriminate` method (line 280) to discriminate the `recognized` variable from among the three possible shapes of our *tool box*. The recognized variable (returned by the **find** method of `GestureDatabase`) is a pair, where the first element is the score of the recognition, and the second element is the actual recognized gesture. We use the second value (`recognized[1]`) for the discrimination process (line 281) and then call the corresponding method (`add_stickman`, `add_line`, and `add_circle`). In the case of lines, it also decides the order in which to send the coordinates to match the direction.

Fourth, the `activate` and `deactivate` methods provide an interface in order to activate or deactivate the *gesture mode* (the application mode in which we can use gestures). To activate the mode, the `activate` method binds the `on_touch_up`, `on_touch_move`, and `on_tourch_down` events to the corresponding up, move, and down methods. It also uses the **disabled** property (lines 238) to disable the *tool box* widget when the gesture mode is on. The `deactivate` method unbinds the events and restores the **disabled** property.

We applied the **disabled** property to the entire `ToolBox` instance, but it automatically looks for the children that belong to it and deactivates them as well. Basically, the event is never sent to the children.

The gestures mode is activated and deactivated from the general options buttons with the gestures `ToggleButton`. We need to change the definition of the `gestures` method in the `generaloptions.py` file:

```
307. def gestures(self, instance, value):
308.     if value == 'down':
309.         self.drawing_space.activate()
310.     else:
311.         self.drawing_space.deactivate()
```

When **gestures** `ToggleButton` is down, then the *gesture mode* is activated; otherwise, the normal functionality of the *tool box* operates.

In the next lesson, we will learn how to enhance the functionality of our widgets using behaviors.

Behaviors – enhancing widget's functionality

Behaviors were introduced recently in the Kivy version 1.8.0, and allow us to increase the functionality and flexibility of the existing widgets. Basically, they let us inject classic behaviors of certain widgets into other behaviors. For example, we can use **ButtonBehavior** in order to add the on_press and on_release functionality to a Label or Image widget. Currently, there are three types of behavior (**ButtonBehavior**, **ToggleButtonBehavior**, and **DragBehavior**) and more will be coming in the next Kivy releases.

Let's add some credits to our application. We want to add some functionality to the *Status Bar* so that when we click, a **Popup** will appear and show some text. First, we will import the necessary components into the statusbar.py header, and also change the class definition of StatusBar:

```
312. # File name: statusbar.py
313. import kivy
314. from kivy.uix.boxlayout import BoxLayout
315. from kivy.properties import NumericProperty, ObjectProperty
316. from kivy.uix.behaviors import ButtonBehavior
317. from kivy.uix.popup import Popup
318. from kivy.uix.label import Label
319.
320. class StatusBar(ButtonBehavior, BoxLayout):
```

In the previous code, we have added the **ButtonBehavior**, **Popup**, and **Label** class (lines 316 and 318). Moreover, we made StatusBar inherit from both ButtonBehavior and BoxLayout at the same time with Python's multiple inheritance. We can add behaviors to any type of widget, and remember from *Chapter 1, GUI Basics – Building an Interface*, that layouts are also widgets. We take advantage of the **ButtonBehavior** that **StatusBar** is inheriting from, in order to use the **on_press** method:

```
321.     def on_press(self):
322.         the_content = Label(text = "Kivy: Interactive Apps
                 and Games in Python\nRoberto Ulloa, Packt
                 Publishing")
323.         the_content.color = (1,1,1,1)
324.         popup = Popup(title='The Comic Creator',
                 content = the_content, size_hint=(None, None),
                 size=(350, 150))
325.         popup.open()
```

We override the **on_press** method to display a **Popup** window on the screen with the credits of the application.

 Notice that behaviors don't change the appearance of the widget; only the functionality that is most often related to processing interactions based upon the users input.

In lines 322 and 323, we create a Label instance with the text we want to show, and make sure that the color is white. In line 324, we create the Popup instance with a title, and the Label instance as content. Finally, in line 325, we display the Popup instance. Here is the result we get after clicking the *Status Bar*:

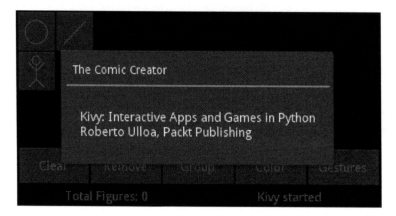

In theory, we can add behaviors to any widget. However, there are practical limitations that could lead to unexpected results. For example, what happens when we add ButtonBehavior to ToggleButton? ToggleButton inherits from Button and Button from ButtonBehavior. As a consequence, we inherit the same method twice. Multiple inheritance is indeed tricky sometimes. This example was obvious (why would we think about making a class that inherits from ButtonBehavior and ToggleButton?). However, there are many other complex widgets that already include functionality for the touch events.

 You should be careful when adding behaviors to widgets that overlap the functionality related to the behaviors. The current behaviors, ButtonBehavior, ToggleButtonBehavior, DragBehavior, CompoundSelectionBehavior, and FocusBehavior are related to touch events.

A special example of this is the `Video` widget, which we will explore in *Chapter 6, Kivy Player – a TED Video Streamer*. This widget has a property called `state`, the same name as the state property of `ToggleButton`. This will cause a name conflict if we want to use multiple inheritances from both classes.

You may have noticed that we set the **Label** color of the label explicitly to white (line 323), which is the label's default color anyway. We did this in order to have everything ready for the next section in which we will decorate our interface.

Style – decorating the interface

In this section, we will redecorate our interface to improve the look and feel of it. With very few strategic changes, we will completely renovate the way our application looks with a few steps. Let's start changing the background color from black to white. We will do this in the `comiccreator.py` file, and here is its new header:

```
326. # File name: comiccreator.py
327. import kivy
328. from kivy.app import App
329. from kivy.lang import Builder
330. from kivy.uix.screenmanager import ScreenManager
331. from kivy.core.window import Window
332.
333. Window.clearcolor = (1, 1, 1, 1)
334.
335. Builder.load_file('style.kv')
```

We imported the **Window** class that manages the configurations of the application window, and controls some global parameters and events, such as the keyboard events, which will be covered in *Chapter 5, Invaders Revenge – an Interactive Multitouch Game*. We use the `Window` class to change the background color of the application to white with the **clearcolor** property (line 333). Finally, we add a new file to `Builder`. The file called `style.kv` is presented here:

```
336. # File name: style.kv
337.
338. <Label>:
339.     bold: True
340.     color: 0,.3,.6,1
341.
```

```
342.  <Button>:
343.      background_normal: 'normal.png'
344.      background_down: 'down.png'
345.      color: 1,1,1,1
```

We need colors that contrast with the white background that we just applied on the entire window. Therefore, we are making changes on two of the basic widgets of Kivy, `Label` and `Button`, and this affects all the components that inherit from them. We have set the **bold** property (line 339) of `Label` to `True`, and set the `color` property (line 340) to blue (gray in the printed version).

We have also changed the default background of the `Button` class and introduced how to create rounded buttons. The **background_normal** property (line 343) indicates the background image that `Button` uses in its normal state, whereas the **background_down** property (line 344) indicates the image that `Button` uses when it is pressed.

Finally, we have reset the `color` property (line 345) of `Button` to white. You may wonder why we did that if the default color of the text of the `Button` class is white. The problem is that we just changed the color of the `Label` class, and, since `Button` inherits from label, the change also affects the `Button` class.

 The order of the rules also matters. If we put the `<Button>:` rule first, then it won't work anymore because the `<Label>:` rule will overwrite the `<Button>:` rule.

We can see the result of our embellished interface:

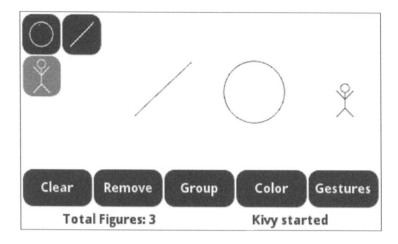

There is still something not quite right with the new design. The lines of our figures are quite thin compared to the rest of the fonts, and somehow the contrast is lost with a white background. Let's learn a quick remedy to change the default properties of our lines.

Factory – replacing a vertex instruction

This final section of this chapter teaches a valuable trick to change the default properties of the **vertex instructions**. We want to change the width of all the lines on our interface. This includes the circles, lines, and stickmen. Of course, we could revisit all the classes that create the Line vertex instructions (remember that the circles are also Line instances, and the stickmen are composed of Line instances as well), and change the width property in all of them. Needless to say, that would be tedious.

Instead, we will replace the default Line class. Indeed, this is equivalent to what we just did in the previous section when we changed the label and button default properties. We have a problem in that we cannot create rules in the Kivy language to change the vertex instructions. But there is an equivalent way around this, using Python code in a new file called style.py:

```
346. # File name: style.py
347. from kivy.graphics import Line
348. from kivy.factory import Factory
349.
350. class NewLine (Line):
351.     def __init__(self, **kwargs):
352.         if not kwargs.get('width'):
353.             kwargs['width'] = 1.5
354.         Line.__init__(self, **kwargs)
355.
356. Factory.unregister('Line')
357. Factory.register('Line', cls=NewLine)
```

In this code, we have created our own NewLine class that inherits from the Kivy Line class (line 350). With a little Python trick, we have changed the kwargs parameter of the constructor method (__init__) in order to set a different default width (line 353). The kwargs parameter is a dictionary that contains all the properties that are explicitly set when a Line instance is created. In this case, if the width property is not indicated in the constructor (line 352), we set the width default to 1.5 (line 353). Then, we call the constructor of the base class with the adjusted kwargs (line 354).

Now, it is time to replace the default Kivy Line class with ours. We need to import the Kivy **Factory** (line 348) that we can use to register or unregister classes, and instance them in the Kivy language. First, we need to unregister the current Line with the **unregister** method (line 356). Then, we need to register our NewLine with the **register** method (line 357). In both methods, the first parameter represents the name that is used to instance the class from the Kivy language. Since we are replacing the class, we will register the NewLine class with the same name. In the **register** method (line 357), the second parameter (cls) indicates the class that we register.

> We could use the **Factory** class to add different lines that we need to constantly use in the Kivy language. For example, we could register our new class with the name ThickLine and then instance it in the Kivy language.

We purposely avoided this strategy, since we actually want to replace the default Line, so we can affect all the Line instances that we create directly in the Kivy language. However, we shouldn't forget to use the NewLine class to create the instances that the user will create dynamically. We need to import NewLine from the style file and set an alias name (Line) so we can reference the class with the same name (line 362). We also need to remove the one we imported from kivy.graphics (line 362) in the toolbox.py file to avoid a name conflict:

```
358. # File name: toolbox.py
359. import math
360. from kivy.uix.togglebutton import ToggleButton
361. from kivy.graphics import Color
362. from style import Line
363. from comicwidgets import StickMan, DraggableWidget
```

Here is the final screenshot of our *Comic Creator*, which shows off the thicker lines:

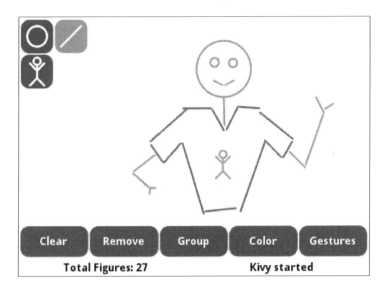

Summary

This chapter covered some specific and useful topics that improve the user experience. We added several screens and switched between them with ScreenManager. We learned how to use colors in the canvas, and we should now have a good understanding of how this works internally. We also learned how to limit the drawing area to the **drawing space** with StencilView. We used Scatter to add rotating and scaling capabilities to DraggableWidget and expanded the functionality through the use of properties and associated events. We also introduced the use of gestures to make the interface more dynamic. We covered how to enhance widget using behaviors. Finally, we learned how to improve the interface by modifying the default widgets and vertex instructions.

Here is a review of all the classes with their respective methods, properties, and attributes that we learned to use in this chapter:

- `ScreenManager`: The `transistion` and `current` properties
- `FadeTransition`, `SwapTransition`, `SlideTransition`, and `WipeTransition` transitions
- `Screen`: The `name` and `manager` properties
- `ColorPicker`: The `color` property
- `StencilView`
- `Scatter`: The `rotate` and `scale` properties, and the `on_translate`, `on_rotate` and `on_scale` methods (events)
- `ScatterLayout`: The `size_hint` and `pos_hint` properties
- `Gesture`: The `add_stroke`, `normalize`, and `rotate` methods
- `GestureDatabase`: The `gesture_to_str`, `str_to_gesture`, `add_gesture`, and `find` methods
- `Widget`: The `disabled` property
- `ButtonBehavior`, `ToggleBehavior` and `DragBehavior`: The `on_press` method
- `Popup`: The `title` and `content` properties
- `Window`: The `clearcolor` attribute
- `Factory`: The `register` and `unregister` methods

These are all useful components that help us create more attractive and dynamic applications. In this chapter, we gave an example on how to demonstrate the possibilities of the classes. Although we didn't exhaustively explore all the options, we should feel comfortable to use any of these components to enhance applications. We can always check the Kivy API for a more comprehensive list of properties and methods.

The next chapter will introduce personalized multi-touch control, animations, as well as the clock and keyboard events. We will create a new interactive project, a game that resembles the Arcade game *Space Invaders*.

5
Invaders Revenge – an Interactive Multi-touch Game

This chapter introduces a collection of components and strategies to make animated and dynamic applications. Most of them are particularly useful for game development. This chapter is full of examples of how to combine different Kivy elements and teaches strategies to control multiple events happening at the same time. The examples are all integrated in a completely new project, a version of the classic *Space Invaders* game (Copyright ©1978 Taito Corporation, http://en.wikipedia.org/wiki/Space_Invaders). The following is a list of the main components that we will work on in this chapter:

- **Atlas**: A Kivy package that allows us to load images efficiently
- **Sound**: Classes that allow sound management
- **Animations**: Transitions, time control, events, and operations that can be applied to animate widgets
- **Clock**: A class that allows us to schedule events
- **Multi-touch**: A strategy that allows us to control different actions according to touches
- **Keyboard**: The Kivy strategy of capturing keyboard events

The first section presents an overview of the project, the GUI, and the rules of the game. After that, we will follow a bottom-up approach. The simple classes that refer to individual components of the game will be explained, and additional topics of the chapter will then be introduced one after another. We will finish with the classes that have the main control over the game. By the end of this chapter, you should be able to start any game application you have always wanted to implement for your mobile device.

Invaders Revenge – an animated multi-touch game

Invaders Revenge is the name of our Kivy version of Space Invaders©. The following screenshot shows you the game we will build in this chapter:

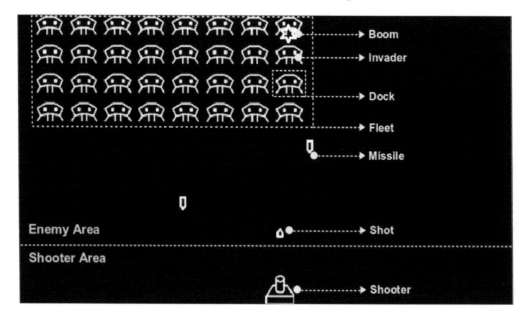

There are several tags in yellow and cyan in the screenshot (or gray dashed lines in the printed version). They help identify the structure of our game; the game will consist of one *shooter* (the player), who shoots (*shots*) at 32 (8x4) *invaders* who are trying to destroy the *shooter* with their *missiles*. The *invaders* are organized in a *fleet* (which moves horizontally) and sometimes an individual *invader* can break out of the grid formation and fly around the screen before going back to its corresponding position (*dock*) in the *fleet*.

The cyan (gray in the printed version) line across the screen indicates an internal division of the screen into the *enemy area* and *shooter area*. This division is used to distinguish between actions that should occur according to touches that happen in different sections of the screen.

The skeleton of the game is presented in the `invasion.kv` file:

```
1.  # File name: invasion.kv
2.  <Invasion>:
3.    id: _invasion
4.    shooter: _shooter
5.    fleet: _fleet
6.    AnchorLayout:
7.      anchor_y: 'top'
8.      anchor_x: 'center'
9.      FloatLayout:
10.       id: _enemy_area
11.       size_hint: 1, .7
12.       Fleet:
13.         id: _fleet
14.         invasion: _invasion
15.         shooter: _shooter
16.         cols: 8
17.         spacing: 40
18.         size_hint: .5, .4
19.         pos_hint: {'top': .9}
20.         x: root.width/2-root.width/4
21.    AnchorLayout:
22.      anchor_y: 'bottom'
23.      anchor_x: 'center'
24.      FloatLayout:
25.        size_hint: 1, .3
26.        Shooter:
27.          id: _shooter
28.          invasion: _invasion
29.          enemy_area: _enemy_area
```

There are two `AnchorLayout` instances. The top one is the *enemy area* that contains the *fleet* and the bottom one is the *shooter area* that contains the *shooter*.

 The *enemy area* and *shooter area* are very important for the logic of the game in order to distinguish between the types of touches on the screen.

We also created some IDs and references that will allow the interaction between different instances of the interface. The following diagram summarizes these relations:

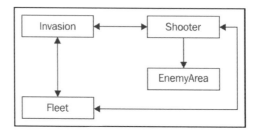

Atlas – An efficient management of images

When it comes to applications that use many images, it is important to reduce their loading time, especially when they are requested from a remote server.

 One strategy to reduce the loading time is to use an **Atlas** (also known as sprite). An Atlas groups all the application images into one big image, so it reduces the number of necessary requests to the operating system, or online requests.

Here is the image of the Atlas we use for invaders revenge:

Instead of requesting five images for the *invaders revenge*, we will just request the Atlas image. We will also need an associated json file that tells us the exact coordinates of each unit in the image. The good news is that we don't need to do this manually. Kivy provides a simple command to create both the Atlas image and the json file. Assuming that all the images are in a directory called img, we just need to open a terminal, go to the img directory (that contains the individual images), and run the following command in the terminal:

```
python -m kivy.atlas invasion 100 *.png
```

In order to execute the previous command, will you need to install the **Pillow library** (http://python-pillow.github.io/).

The command contains three parameters, namely **basename**, **size**, and **images list**. The basename parameter is the prefix of the json file (img/invasion.json) and the Atlas image or images (img/invasion-0.png). It could happen that several Atlas images are generated, in which case we would have several images with basename as a prefix followed by a numerical identifier, for example, invasion-0.png and invasion-1.png. The size parameter indicates the size in pixels of the resulting Atlas image. Be sure to specify a size that is larger than the biggest of the images. The **image list** parameter is the list of all the images that will be added to the Atlas, and we can use the * wildcard. In our case, we will use it to indicate all files with the .png extension.

In order to use the Atlas in the Kivy language, we have to use the following format: atlas://path/to/atlas/atlas_name/id. The id file refers to the image filename without the extension. For example, normally we would have referenced the *shooter* image as a source: 'img/shooter.png'. After generating the Atlas, it becomes source: 'atlas://images/invasion/shooter'. The following image.kv file presents the code for all the images of *Invaders Revenge*:

```
30. # File name: images.kv
31. <Invader>:
32.    source: 'atlas://img/invasion/invader'
33.    size_hint: None,None
34.    size: 40,40
35. <Shooter>:
36.    source: 'atlas://img/invasion/shooter'
37.    size_hint: None,None
38.    size: 40,40
39.    pos: self.parent.width/2, 0
40. <Boom>:
41.    source: 'atlas://img/invasion/boom'
42.    size_hint: None,None
43.    size: 26,30
44. <Shot>:
45.    source: 'atlas://img/invasion/shot'
46.    size_hint: None,None
47.    size: 12,15
48. <Missile>:
49.    source: 'atlas://img/invasion/missile'
50.    size_hint: None,None
51.    size: 12,27
```

All the classes in this file inherit, directly or indirectly, from the `Image` class. The `Missile` and `Shot` inherit first from the class called `Ammo`, which also inherits from `Image`. There is also the `Boom` class that will create the effect of an explosion when any `Ammo` is triggered. Apart from the `Boom` image (a star in the Atlas), the `Boom` class will be associated with a sound that we will add in the next section.

Boom – simple sound effects

Adding sound effects in Kivy is very simple. A `Boom` instance will produce a sound when it is created, and this will happen every time a *shot* or *missile* is fired. Here is the code for `boom.py`:

```
52. # File name: boom.py
53. from kivy.uix.image import Image
54. from kivy.core.audio import SoundLoader
55.
56. class Boom(Image):
57.     sound = SoundLoader.load('boom.wav')
58.     def boom(self, **kwargs):
59.         self.__class__.sound.play()
60.         super(Boom, self).__init__(**kwargs)
```

Reproducing a sound involves the use of two classes, **Sound** and **SoundLoader** (line 54). `SoundLoader` loads an audio file (`.wav`) and returns a `Sound` instance (line 57) that we keep in the `sound` reference (a static attribute of the `Boom` class). We play a sound every time a new `Boom` instance is created.

Ammo – simple animation

This section explains how to animate *shots* and *missiles*, which show very similar behavior. They move from their original position to a destination, constantly checking whether a target has been hit. The following is the code for the `ammo.py` class:

```
61. # File name: ammo.py
62. from kivy.animation import Animation
63. from kivy.uix.image import Image
64. from boom import Boom
65.
66. class Ammo(Image):
67.     def shoot(self, tx, ty, target):
68.         self.target = target
```

```
69.       self.animation = Animation(x=tx, top=ty)
70.       self.animation.bind(on_start = self.on_start)
71.       self.animation.bind(on_progress = self.on_progress)
72.       self.animation.bind(on_complete = self.on_stop)
73.       self.animation.start(self)
74.
75.    def on_start(self, instance, value):
76.       self.boom = Boom()
77.       self.boom.center=self.center
78.       self.parent.add_widget(self.boom)
79.
80.    def on_progress(self, instance, value, progression):
81.       if progression >= .1:
82.          self.parent.remove_widget(self.boom)
83.       if self.target.collide_ammo(self):
84.          self.animation.stop(self)
85.
86.    def on_stop(self, instance,value):
87.       self.parent.remove_widget(self)
88.
89. class Shot(Ammo):
90.    pass
91. class Missile(Ammo):
92.    pass
```

For the Ammo animation, we require a simple **Animation** (line 69). We send x and top as parameters.

 The parameters of an Animation instance can be any properties of the widget to which we are applying the animation.

In this case, the x and top properties belong to Ammo itself. This is enough to set Animation of Ammo from its original position to tx, ty.

 By default, the execution period of **Animation** is one second.

We need Ammo to do a few more things in its trajectory.

 The Animation class includes three events, which are triggered when the animations starts (**on_start**), during its progress (**on_progress**), and when it stops (**on_stop**).

We bind these events (lines 70 to 72) to our own methods. The **on_start** method (line 75) displays a Boom instance (line 76) when the animation starts. The **on_progress** (lines 80 to 84) method removes Boom after 10 percent of **progression** (lines 81 and 82). Also, it is constantly checking target (line 83). When target is hit, the animation is stopped (line 84). Once the animation ends (or is stopped), Ammo is removed from the parent (line 82).

Lines 89 to 92 define two classes, Shot and Missile. The Shot and Missile classes inherit from Ammo and their only difference right now is the image that is used in images.kv. Eventually, we will use Shot instances for the *shooter*, and Missile instances for the *invaders*. Before this, let's give the *invaders* some freedom, so they can leave their *fleet* and perform an individual attack.

Invader – transitions for animations

The previous section uses the default Animation transition. This is a Linear transition, which means that the Widget instance moves from one point to another in a straight line. *Invaders* trajectories can be more interesting. For example, there could be accelerations, or changes of direction, as shown by the line in the following screenshot:

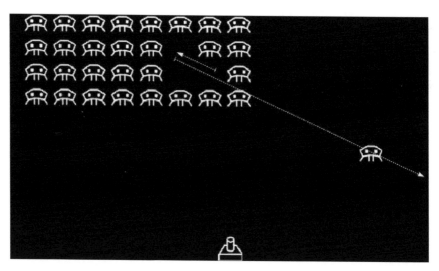

The following is the code of `invader.py`:

```
93.  # File name: invader.py
94.  from kivy.core.window import Window
95.  from kivy.uix.image import Image
96.  from kivy.animation import Animation
97.  from random import choice, randint
98.  from ammo import Missile
99.
100. class Invader(Image):
101.     pre_fix = ['in_','out_','in_out_']
102.     functions = ['back','bounce','circ','cubic',
103.        'elastic','expo','quad','quart','quint','sine']
104.     formation = True
105.
106.     def solo_attack(self):
107.       if self.formation:
108.         self.parent.unbind_invader()
109.         animation = self.trajectory()
110.         animation.bind(on_complete = self.to_dock)
111.         animation.start(self)
112.
113.     def trajectory(self):
114.       fleet = self.parent.parent
115.       area = fleet.parent
116.       x = choice((-self.width,area.width+self.width))
117.       y = randint(round(area.y), round(fleet.y))
118.       t = choice(self.pre_fix) + choice(self.functions)
119.       return Animation(x=x, y=y,d=randint(2,7),t=t)
120.
121.     def to_dock(self, instance, value):
122.       self.y = Window.height
123.       self.center_x = Window.width/2
124.       animation = Animation(pos=self.parent.pos, d=2)
125.       animation.bind(on_complete =
                self.parent.bind_invader)
126.       animation.start(self)
127.
128.     def drop_missile(self):
129.       missile = Missile()
```

```
130.        missile.center = (self.center_x, self.y)
131.        fleet = self.parent.parent
132.        fleet.invasion.add_widget(missile)
133.        missile.shoot(self.center_x,0,fleet.shooter)
```

The idea behind this code is to let an *invader* break the formation from the *fleet* and proceed into a `solo_attack` (lines 106 to 111) method. The *invader's* `Animation` is created in the `trajectory` method (lines 113 and 119) by randomizing the final point of the *invader's* trajectory (lines 116 and 117). This randomization will pick up two coordinates on the left or right borders of the *enemy area*. Also, we randomize the type of **transition** (line 118), and **duration** (line 119) to create more diverse and unpredictable trajectories.

Kivy currently includes 31 **transitions**. They are represented by a string such as `'in_out_cubic'`, where `in_out` is a prefix that describes the way in which the function (`cubic`) is used. There are three possible prefixes (`in`, `out`, and `in_out`), and 10 functions (line 102), such as `cubic`, `exponential`, `sin`, `quadratic`. Please visit the Kivy API for a description of all of them (`http://kivy.org/docs/api-kivy.animation.html`).

Line 118 selects one of the transitions randomly. The transition is applied to the progress, and therefore to `x` and `y` at the same time, which produces an interesting acceleration effect on the trajectories.

When the `Animation` class ends its trajectory (line 110), the `to_dock` method (lines 121 to 126) brings the *invader* back to its original position starting from the top-center part of `Window`. We use the **Window** class to get `height` and `width`. Sometimes this is easier than traversing the chain of parents, to find the root widget. When the *invader* reaches the *dock*, it is bound back to it (line 125).

The last method (`drop_missile` in lines 128 to 133) shoots one *missile* that follows a vertical line starting from the *invader's* bottom-center position (line 130) to the bottom of the screen (line 133). Remember that the `Missile` class inherits from the `Ammo` class we created in the previous section.

Our invaders can now move freely around the enemy area. However, we would also like to have some sort of group movement. In the next section, we will create a *dock* for each corresponding invader. In this way, the *invader* has a corresponding placeholder in the *fleet* formation. After this, we will create the *fleet*, which constantly moves all the *docks*.

Dock – automatic binding in the Kivy language

You might realize from previous chapters that the Kivy language does more than simply transform its rules to Python instructions. For instance, you might see that when it creates properties, it also binds them.

 When we do something common such as `pos: self.parent.pos` inside a layout, then the property of the parent is bound to its child. The child always moves to the parent position when the parent moves.

This is usually desirable but not all the time. Think about `solo_attack` of the *invader*. We need it to break formation and follow a free trajectory on the screen. While this happens, the whole formation of *invaders* continues moving from right to left and vice versa. This means that the *invader* will receive two orders at the same time; one from the moving parent and another from the trajectory's `Animation`.

This means that we need a placeholder (the *dock*) for each *invader*. This will secure the space for the *invader* when it comes back from executing a solo attack. If we don't have a placeholder, the layout (`GridLayout`, as we will see in the next section) of the *fleet* will automatically reconfigure the formation, reallocating the rest of the *invaders* to fill the empty space. Also, the *invader* needs to free itself from the parent (the *dock*) so it can float to any location on the screen. The following code (`dock.py`) binds (lines 145 to 147) and unbinds (lines 149 to 151) the *invader* using Python, and not the Kivy language:

```
134. # File name: dock.py
135. from kivy.uix.widget import Widget
136. from invader import Invader
137.
138. class Dock(Widget):
139.   def __init__(self, **kwargs):
140.     super(Dock, self).__init__(**kwargs)
141.     self.invader = Invader()
142.     self.add_widget(self.invader)
143.     self.bind_invader()
144.
145.   def bind_invader(self, instance=None, value=None):
146.     self.invader.formation = True
```

```
147.        self.bind(pos = self.on_pos)
148.
149.    def unbind_invader(self):
150.        self.invader.formation = False
151.        self.unbind(pos = self.on_pos)
152.
153.    def on_pos(self, instance, value):
154.        self.invader.pos = self.pos
```

 We use the knowledge from *Chapter 3, Widget Events – Binding Actions*, for this code, but the important part is the strategy that we apply.

There will be situations in which we will want to avoid using the Kivy language because it is preferable to have complete control.

This doesn't mean that it is impossible to solve this using the Kivy language. For example, one common approach is to switch the *invader's* parent (*dock*) to, let's say, the root `Widget` instance of the application; this unbinds the position of the *invader* from its current parent. It doesn't really matter which approach we follow. As long as we understand the mechanisms, we will be able to find elegant solutions.

Now that each invader has a *dock* securing its place in the *invaders* formation, we are ready to introduce some movement to the *fleet*.

Fleet – infinite concatenation of animations

In this section, we will animate the fleet so that it has perpetual movement from right to left and vice versa, as shown by the arrows in the following screenshot:

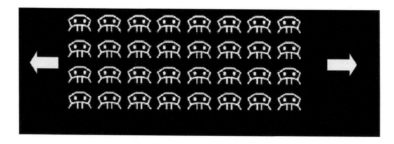

In order to do this, we will learn how to concatenate one animation just after another one is completed. Indeed, we will create an infinite loop of animations so that the *fleet* is in perpetual movement.

 We can concatenate two animations with the on_complete event.

The following code, fragment 1 (of 2), of fleet.py shows how to concatenate these events:

```
155. # File name: fleet.py (Fragment 1)
156. from kivy.uix.gridlayout import GridLayout
157. from kivy.properties import ListProperty
158. from kivy.animation import Animation
159. from kivy.clock import Clock
160. from kivy.core.window import Window
161. from random import randint, random
162. from dock import Dock
163.
164. class Fleet(GridLayout):
165.    survivors = ListProperty(())
166.
167.    def __init__(self, **kwargs):
168.       super(Fleet, self).__init__(**kwargs)
169.       for x in range(0, 32):
170.          dock = Dock()
171.          self.add_widget(dock)
172.          self.survivors.append(dock)
173.       self.center_x= Window.width/4
174.
175.    def start_attack(self, instance, value):
176.       self.invasion.remove_widget(value)
177.       self.go_left(instance, value)
178.       self.schedule_events()
179.
180.    def go_left(self, instance, value):
181.       animation = Animation(x = 0)
182.       animation.bind(on_complete = self.go_right)
183.       animation.start(self)
184.
185.    def go_right(self, instance, value):
186.       animation = Animation(right=self.parent.width)
187.       animation.bind(on_complete = self.go_left)
188.       animation.start(self)
```

The `go_left` method (lines 180 to 183) binds the `on_complete` (line 182) event of an `Animation` instance to the `go_right` method (lines 185 to 188). Similarly, the `go_right` method binds the `on_complete` (line 187) event of another `Animation` instance to the `go_left` method. With this strategy, we create an infinite loop of two animations.

The `fleet.py` class also overloads the constructor to add 32 *invaders* (lines 169 to 173) to the children of `Fleet`. These *invaders* are added to the survivors **ListProperty** that we use to keep track of the *invaders* that haven't been shot down. The `start_attack` method (lines 175 to 178) starts the `Fleet` animation calling the `go_left` method (line 177) and the `schedule_events` method (line 178). The latter makes use of `Clock`, which will be explained in the next section.

Scheduling events with the clock

We saw that `Animation` has a duration parameter that establishes the time in which an animation should take place. A different time-related topic is the scheduling of a particular task at a certain time or during intervals of n seconds. In these cases, we use the **Clock** class. Let's analyze the following code, fragment 2 (of 2), of `fleet.py`:

```
189. # File name: fleet.py (Fragment 2)
190.    def schedule_events(self):
191.       Clock.schedule_interval(self.solo_attack, 2)
192.       Clock.schedule_once(self.shoot, random())
193.
194.    def solo_attack(self, dt):
195.       if len(self.survivors):
196.          rint = randint(0, len(self.survivors) - 1)
197.          child = self.survivors[rint]
198.          child.invader.solo_attack()
199.
200.    def shoot(self, dt):
201.       if len(self.survivors):
202.          rint = randint(0, len(self.survivors) - 1)
203.          child = self.survivors[rint]
204.          child.invader.drop_missile()
205.          Clock.schedule_once(self.shoot, random())
206.
207.    def collide_ammo(self, ammo):
208.       for child in self.survivors:
```

```
209.          if child.invader.collide_widget(ammo):
210.              child.canvas.clear()
211.              self.survivors.remove(child)
212.              return True
213.      return False
214.
215.  def on_survivors(self, instance, value):
216.      if len(self.survivors) == 0:
217.          Clock.unschedule(self.solo_attack)
218.          Clock.unschedule(self.shoot)
219.          self.invasion.end_game("You Win!")
```

The schedule_events method (lines 190 to 192) schedules actions for a particular time. Line 191 schedules the solo_attack method every two seconds. Line 192 schedules shoot just once at random (between 0 and 1) seconds.

> The **schedule_interval** method schedules actions periodically, whereas the **schedule_once** method schedules an action just once.

The solo_attack method (lines 194 to 198) randomly selects one of the survivors to perform the solo attack that we studied for the *invaders* (lines 106 to 111 of invader. py). The shoot method (lines 200 to 205) randomly selects one survivor to fire a *missile* at the *shooter* (lines 201 to 204). After this, the method schedules another shoot (line 205).

In the Ammo class, we used the collide_ammo method to verify that an Ammo instance hits any of the *invaders* (line 83 of ammo.py). Now, in fleet.py, we implemented such a method (lines 207 or 213) that hides and removes the *invader* from the survivors list. The on_survivors event is triggered every time we modify the survivors ListProperty. When there are no survivors left, we unschedule the events with the **unscheduled** method (lines 217 and 218) and end the game by displaying the **You Win!** message.

We finished creating the shooter enemies. Now it is time to provide the *shooter* with movement to dodge the *missiles* and *shots* to hit the *invaders*.

Shooter – multi-touch control

Kivy supports multi-touch interactions. This feature is always present but we haven't paid too much attention to it except when we used the `Scatter` widget in *Chapter 4, Improving the User Experience*. Additionally, we didn't clarify that the entire screen and GUI components are already capable of multi-touch, and that Kivy handles the events accordingly.

 Kivy handles multi-touch actions internally. This means that all the Kivy widgets and components support multi-touch interaction; we don't have to worry about it. Kivy solves all the possible conflicts of ambiguous situations that are common in multi-touch control, for example, touching two buttons at the same time.

That said, it is up to us to control particular implementations. Multi-touch programming introduces logic problems that we need to solve as developers. Nevertheless, Kivy provides the data related to each particular touch so we can work on the logic. The main problem is that we need to constantly distinguish one touch from another, and then take the respective actions.

With Invaders Revenge, we need to distinguish between two actions that are triggered by the same type of touch. The first action is the *shooter's* horizontal movement in order to avoid the invaders' *missiles*. The second is touching the screen to fire at the *invaders*. The following screenshot illustrates these two actions with the wide thick arrows (sliding touch) and the dotted thin arrow (shot action):

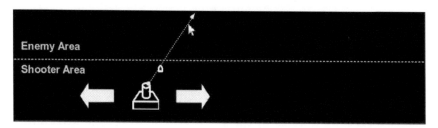

The following code, fragment 1 (of 2), of `shooter.py` controls these two actions by using the *enemy area* and *shooter area*:

```
220. # File name: shooter.py (Fragment 1)
221. from kivy.clock import Clock
222. from kivy.uix.image import Image
```

```
223. from ammo import Shot
224.
225. class Shooter(Image):
226.    reloaded = True
227.    alife = False
228.
229.    def on_touch_down(self, touch):
230.       if self.parent.collide_point(*touch.pos):
231.          self.center_x = touch.x
232.          touch.ud['move'] = True
233.       elif self.enemy_area.collide_point(*touch.pos):
234.          self.shoot(touch.x,touch.y)
235.          touch.ud['shoot'] = True
236.
237.    def on_touch_move(self, touch):
238.       if self.parent.collide_point(*touch.pos):
239.          self.center_x = touch.x
240.       elif self.enemy_area.collide_point(*touch.pos):
241.          self.shoot(touch.x,touch.y)
242.
243.    def on_touch_up(self, touch):
244.       if 'shoot' in touch.ud and touch.ud['shoot']:
245.          self.reloaded = True
```

The on_touch_down (lines 229 to 235) and on_touch_move (lines 237 to 241) methods distinguish between the two actions, *movement* or *shoot*, by using the *shooter area* (lines 230 and 238) and the *enemy area* (lines 233 and 240) widgets, respectively, in order to collide the coordinates of the event.

The touch coordinates are the most common strategy to identify specific touches. However, touches have many other attributes that could help to distinguish between them, for example, timing, a double (or triple) tap, or the input device. You can check the MotionEvent class to review all the attributes of a touch (http://kivy.org/docs/api-kivy.input.motionevent.html#kivy.input.motionevent.MotionEvent).

In contrast, the on_touch_up method (line 243) follows a different approach. It uses the **ud** attribute (user data dictionary to store personalized data on the touch) of a MotionEvent instance (touch) to determine whether the touchdown that started the event was a *movement* (in the *shooter area*) or a *shoot* (in the *enemy area*). We set touch.ud (lines 232 and 235) previously on on_touch_down.

 Kivy keeps the touch event associated with the three basic touch events (down, move, and up), so the touch references we get for on_touch_down, on_touch_move, and on_touch_up are the same, and we can distinguish between touches.

Let's now analyze the details of the methods that are called on by these events. The following is the code, fragment 2 (of 2), of shooter.py:

```
246.  # File name: shooter.py (Fragment 2)
247.    def start(self, instance, value):
248.      self.alife=True
249.
250.    def shoot(self, fx, fy):
251.      if self.reloaded and self.alife:
252.        self.reloaded = False
253.        Clock.schedule_once(self.reload_gun, .5)
254.        shot = Shot()
255.        shot.center = (self.center_x, self.top)
256.        self.invasion.add_widget(shot)
257.        (fx,fy) =
                self.project(self.center_x,self.top,fx,fy)
258.        shot.shoot(fx,fy,self.invasion.fleet)
259.
260.    def reload_gun(self, dt):
261.      self.reloaded = True
262.
263.    def collide_ammo(self, ammo):
264.      if self.collide_widget(ammo) and self.alife:
265.        self.alife = False
266.        self.color = (0,0,0,0)
267.        self.invasion.end_game("Game Over")
268.        return True
```

```
269.       return False
270.
271.    def project(self,ix,iy,fx,fy):
272.       (w,h) = self.invasion.size
273.       if ix == fx: return (ix, h)
274.       m = (fy-iy) / (fx-ix)
275.       b = iy - m*ix
276.       x = (h-b)/m
277.       if x < 0: return (0, b)
278.       elif x > w: return (w, m*w+b)
279.       return (x, h)
```

We first created a method to start the shooter by bringing it to life (line 247 and 248), which we will use when we start the game. Then, we implement an interesting behavior for the on_touch_move method with the shoot method (lines 250 to 258). Instead of shooting as fast as possible, we delay the next shoot by 0.5 seconds. This delay simulates a time lapse in which the gun needs to be reloaded (line 253). Otherwise, it would be unfair to the *invaders* to shoot as fast as the computer allows. Conversely, when we use the on_touch_up method, the gun is reloaded immediately so, in this case, it would be the skill of the player who could fire faster with a touchdown and touch-up sequence.

The collide_ammo method (lines 263 to 269) is almost equivalent to the collide_ammo method of the Fleet (lines 207 to 213). The only difference is that there is just one *shooter* instead of a set of *invaders*. If the *shooter* is hit, then the game is over and the message **Game Over** is displayed. Notice that we don't remove the *shooter*, we simply set its alife flag to False (line 265), and hide it by setting the color to black (line 266). With this, we avoid inconsistencies in references that point to an instance that no longer exists in the interface context.

The project method (lines 271 to 278) extends (project) the touch coordinates to the border of the screen, so the *shot* will continue its trajectory until it reaches the end of the screen and not stop exactly at the touch coordinate. The mathematical details are beyond the scope of this book but it is a simple linear projection.

The application is almost ready. There is just one minor problem. If you don't have a multi-touch screen, you would actually not be able to play this game. The next section introduces how to handle keyboard events in order to have a more classic gaming approach, which combines the keyboard and mouse.

Invasion – moving the shooter with the keyboard

This section offers a second possibility of how to move the *shooter*. If you don't have a multi-touch device, you will need to use something else to control the position of the *shooter* easily while you use the mouse to shoot. The following is the code, fragment 1, (of 2) of `main.py`:

```
280. # File name: main.py (Fragment 1)
281. from kivy.app import App
282. from kivy.lang import Builder
283. from kivy.core.window import Window
284. from kivy.uix.floatlayout import FloatLayout
285. from kivy.uix.label import Label
286. from kivy.animation import Animation
287. from kivy.clock import Clock
288. from fleet import Fleet
289. from shooter import Shooter
290.
291. Builder.load_file('images.kv')
292.
293. class Invasion(FloatLayout):
294.
295.    def __init__(self, **kwargs):
296.       super(Invasion, self).__init__(**kwargs)
297.       self._keyboard = Window.request_keyboard(self.close,
               self)
298.       self._keyboard.bind(on_key_down=self.press)
399.       self.start_game()
300.
301.    def close(self):
302.       self._keyboard.unbind(on_key_down=self.press)
303.       self._keyboard = None
304.
305.    def press(self, keyboard, keycode, text, modifiers):
306.       if keycode[1] == 'left':
307.          self.shooter.center_x -= 30
308.       elif keycode[1] == 'right':
309.          self.shooter.center_x += 30
```

```
310.        return True
311.
312.    def start_game(self):
313.        label = Label(text='Ready!')
314.        animation = Animation (font_size = 72, d=2)
315.        animation.bind(on_complete=self.fleet.start_attack)
316.        animation.bind(on_complete=self.shooter.start)
317.        self.add_widget(label)
318.        animation.start(label)
```

The preceding code illustrates the keyboard event control. The __init__ constructor (lines 295 to 299) will request **keyboard** (line 297) to the Window and bind (line 298) the **on_keyboard_down** event to the **press** method. One important parameter of the Window._request_keyboard method is the method that is called when keyboard is closed (lines 301 to 303). There are many reasons why the keyboard can become closed, including when another widget requests it. The press method (lines 305 to 310) is the one in charge of handling the keyboard input, the pressed key. The pressed key is kept in the keycode parameter and it is used in lines 306 and 308 to decide whether the *shooter* should move left or right.

 The keyboard binding in the game is for testing purposes on devices that have no multi-touch functionality. If you want to try it on your mobile device, you should comment out lines 297 and 298 to deactivate the keyboard binding.

Line 299 calls the start_game method (lines 312 to 318). The method displays Label with the text **Ready!** Notice that we applied an Animation instance to font_size in line 314. So far, we have been using the animations to move widgets around with the x, y, or pos properties. However, animations work with any property (that supports arithmetic operators; as a counter example, String doesn't support such operations). For example, we could use them to animate the rotation or scaling of Scatter. When the animation is complete, it will start both the *fleet* and the *shooter* (lines 315 and 316). Notice how we just bound two methods to the same event.

 There is no limit to the number of methods that we can bind to an event.

In the next section, we will discuss how to animate multiple properties in a sequence or simultaneously.

Combining animations with '+' and '&'

You already learned that you can add several properties to the same animation so that they are modified together (line 69 of `ammo.py`).

 We can combine animations by using the + and & **operators**. The + operator is used to create sequenced animations (one after another). The & operator lets us execute two animations at the same time.

The following code is fragment 2 of `main.py`, and illustrates the use of these two operators:

```
319. # File name: main.py (Fragment 2)
320.   def end_game(self, message):
321.      label = Label(markup=True, size_hint = (.2, .1),
322.         pos=(0,self.parent.height/2), text = message)
323.      self.add_widget(label)
324.      self.composed_animation().start(label)
325.
326.   def composed_animation(self):
327.      animation = Animation (center=self.parent.center)
328.      animation &= Animation (font_size = 72, d=3)
329.      animation += Animation(font_size = 24,y=0,d=2)
330.      return animation
331.
332. class InvasionApp(App):
333.   def build(self):
334.      return Invasion()
335.
336. if __name__=="__main__":
337.    InvasionApp().run()
```

The `end_game` method (lines 320 to 324) displays a final message to indicate how the game ended (**You Win** on line 219 of `fleet.py` or **Game Over** on line 267 of `shooter.py`). This method uses the `composed_animation` method (lines 326 to 330) to create a composed `Animation`, in which we use all the possibilities to combine animations. Line 327 is a simple `Animation` that is joined (with the '&' operator) to execute at the same time with another simple `Animation` of a different duration (line 328). In line 329, an `Animation` containing two properties (`font_size` and `y`) is attached to the previous one with the '+' operator.

The resulting animation does the following: it takes one second to move the message from the left to the middle, while the font size increases in size. When it gets to the middle, the increase in the font size continues for two more seconds. Once the font reaches its full size (72 points), the message moves to the bottom and keeps decreasing in size at the same time. The following diagram illustrates the whole animation sequence:

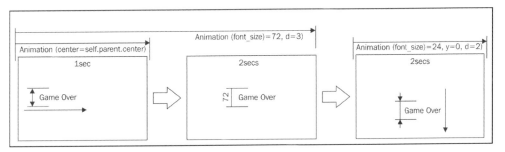

The '+' operator is similar to what we did when we bound the `Animation` `on_complete` event to a method that creates another `Animation` in the *invader*: `animation.bind(on_complete = self.to_dock)` (line 110 of `invader.py`). The difference is that when we use the '+' operator, there is no chance to create an infinite loop as we did with the *fleet*, or change the `Widget` properties before starting another animation. For example, in the *invader* case, we relocated the *invader* to the top-center (lines 122 and 123) of the screen before the animation that carries it back to the *dock* (lines 124 to 126):

```
121.    def to_dock(self, instance, value):
122.      self.y = Window.height
123.      self.center_x = Window.width/2
124.      animation = Animation(pos=self.parent.pos, d=2)
125.      animation.bind(on_complete =
              self.parent.bind_invader)
126.      animation.start(self)
```

The & operator is similar to sending two properties as parameters of the `Animation`, as we did in line 69: `self.animation = Animation(x=tx, top=ty)`. The difference in sending two properties as parameters is that they share the same duration and transition, whereas in line 328, we change the duration of the second property.

Here is one last screenshot that shows how the invaders have finally taken their revenge:

Summary

This chapter covered the whole construction process of an interactive and animated application. You learned how to integrate various Kivy components and you should now be able to comfortably build a 2D animated game.

Let's review all the new classes and components we used in this chapter:

- `Atlas`
- `Image`: The `source` property
- `SoundLoader` and `Sound`: The `load` and `play` methods, respectively
- `Window`: The `height` and `width` properties, and the `request_keyboard`, `remove_widget`, and `add_widget` methods

- `Animation`: The properties as parameters; `d` and `t` parameters; `start`, `stop`, and `bind` methods; `on_start`, `on_progress`, and `on_complete` events; and `'+'` and `'&'` operators

- `Touch`: `ud` attribute

- `Clock`: `schedule_interval` and `schedule_once` methods

- `Keyboard`: `bind` and `unbind` methods, `on_key_down` event

The information contained in this chapter presents tools and strategies you can use to develop highly interactive applications. By combining the previous chapters information with this chapter's insights into the use of properties, binding events, and further understanding of the Kivy language, you should be able to quickly start using all the other components of the Kivy API (`http://kivy.org/docs/api-kivy.html`).

The last chapter, *Chapter 6, Kivy Player – a TED Video Streamer,* of this book will teach you how to control multimedia components, in particular video and audio. It will present another example in order to present a few more Kivy components, but more importantly, it will teach you how to build a more professional looking interface. It will also introduce some Kivy tools to debug our applications.

6
Kivy Player – a TED Video Streamer

In this chapter, we will learn how to search, display, and control videos. We will integrate knowledge from previous chapters to build a responsive application with the ability to adjust to different screens and maximize the use of space. We will produce an enhanced **video** widget with controls and subtitle support, and learn how to display a search result query from the TED API services (`developer.ted.com`). Here are the main topics that we will cover in this chapter:

- Control the progression of a streamed video
- Use the progression of a video to display subtitles at the right moment
- Apply strategies and components to make our application responsive
- Display and navigate a local file directory tree
- Use the Kivy inspector to debug our applications
- Add scroll functionality to a list of results obtained from an Internet query

This chapter wraps up a lot of knowledge acquired so far. We will be reviewing and combining the use of properties, events, animations, touches, behaviors, layouts, and even graphics. At the same time, we will introduce new widgets that will complement your knowledge, and serve as good examples of new programming situations. We will also review the Kivy inspector that will help us detect GUI bugs. At the end of this chapter, we will finish with a professional looking interface.

Video – play, pause, and stop

We will start with simple code in this section, and then gradually include functionality until we get a complete video player. In this section, we will discuss how to use the **Video** widget in order to stream a *video* from the Internet. Let's start with the code in the video.kv file:

```
1. # File name: video.kv
2. #:set _default_video
       "http://video.ted.com/talk/stream/2004/None/
       DanGilbert_2004-180k.mp4"
3.
4. <Video>:
5.     allow_stretch: True
6.     color: 0,0,0,0
7.     source: _default_video
```

In this code, we initially create a constant value with the **set** directive (line 2). This directive allows us to have global values that we can use inside the Kivy language scope. For example, we set the source property of the Video class with the value of the _default_video constant (line 7).

We set up three properties for the **Video** class. The **allow_stretch** property (line 5) allows the video to stretch according to the screen size available. The **color** property (line 6) will tint the video black, to serve as a foreground when the *video* is not playing (and a background for the *cover* image). The **source** property (line 7) contains the URL (or filename) of the video we want to play. These three properties actually belong to the **Image** widget, which is the base class for Video. This makes sense if we think of a video as a sequence of images (accompanied by a sound).

For test purposes, if you want to avoid constantly downloading the video from the Internet (or if the URL is not available anymore), you can replace the URL in default_video with a sample file that is included with the code: samples/BigBuckBunny.ogg.

We will use the **Factory** class to use the technique that we learned about in *Chapter 4, Improving the User Experience*. Back then, we used the **Factory** class to replace the Line vertex instruction with our personalized implementation, a ticker Line.

The **Factory** class follows an oriented-object software design pattern called a factory pattern. A factory pattern returns default new objects (instances) of a subset of classes according to the called identifier, usually a method, but in the case of the Kivy languate we just use a name. (http://en.wikipedia.org/wiki/Factory_%28object-oriented_programming%29).

We will do something similar now, but this time we will personalize our Video **widget**:

```
8.  # File name: video.py
9.  from kivy.uix.video import Video as KivyVideo
10.
11. from kivy.factory import Factory
12. from kivy.lang import Builder
13.
14. Builder.load_file('video.kv')
15.
16. class Video(KivyVideo):
17.
18.     def on_state(self, instance, value):
19.         if self.state == 'stop':
20.             self.seek(0)
21.         return super(self.__class__, self).on_state(instance,
            value)
22.
23.     def on_eos(self, instance, value):
24.         if value:
25.             self.state = 'stop'
26.
27.     def _on_load(self, *largs):
28.         super(self.__class__, self)._on_load(largs)
29.         self.color = (1,1,1,1)
30.
31.     def on_source(self, instance, value):
32.         self.color = (0, 0, 0, 0)
33.
34. Factory.unregister('Video')
35. Factory.register('Video', cls=Video)
```

The `video.py` file will import the Kivy `Video` widget with an alias name `KivyVideo` (line 9). We will now be able to create our personalized widget (lines 16 to 32) using the `Video` class name and not a less attractive alternative name such as `MyVideo`. At the end of the file, we replace the default `Video` widget with our personalized `Video` to the `Factory` (lines 34 and 35). From now on, the referenced `Video` class in the Kivy language will correspond to our implementation in this file.

We created four methods (**on_state, on_eos, _on_load,** and **on_source**) in the `Video` class. All of them correspond to events:

- The **on_state** method (line 18) is called when the state of the *video* changes among its three possible states: playing (`'play'`), paused (`'pause'`), or stopped (`'stop'`). We make sure that when the video is stopped, it is repositioned at the beginning with the **seek** method (line 20).

- The **on_eos** method (line 23) will be called when the **end of stream** (EOS) has been reached. We will make sure that the state is set to `stop` when this occurs (line 19).

- We also need to remember that we tinted the video with black color using the `color` property in the Kivy language (line 6). Therefore, we need to put light (`1,1,1,1`) on the video in order to be able to see it (line 29). The method **_on_load** (line 27) is called when the video is loaded into memory and ready to play. We use this method in order to set the proper (and original Kivy default) `color` property.

> Remember in *Chapter 2, Graphics – the Canvas* that the `color` property of an `Image` widget (base class of the `Video` class) acts as a tint or light over the display. The same effect occurs for the `Video` widget.

- Finally, the **on_source** method, also inherited from the `Image` class, will restore the black tint on top of the video when the source of the video is changed.

Let's proceed to create a `kivyplayer.py` file to execute our application, and also play, pause, and stop our video:

```
36. # File name: kivyplayer.py
37. from kivy.app import App
38.
39. from video import Video
40.
```

```
41. class KivyPlayerApp(App):
42.
43.     def build(self):
44.         self.video = Video()
45.         self.video.bind(on_touch_down=self.touch_down)
46.         return self.video
47.
48.     def touch_down(self, instance, touch):
49.         if self.video.state == 'play':
50.             self.video.state = 'pause'
51.         else:
52.             self.video.state = 'play'
53.         if touch.is_double_tap:
54.             self.video.state = 'stop'
55.
56. if __name__ == "__main__":
57.     KivyPlayerApp().run()
```

For now, we will control the video with touches. In the `build` method (line 43), we have bound the `on_touch_down` event (line 45) of the video to the `touch_down` method (lines 48 to 54). One touch will play or pause the video according to its current **state** property (lines 49 and 52). The state property controls whether the video is in one of three possible states. If it is playing, it will pause it; otherwise (paused or stopped), it will play it. We will use the **double_tap** key that indicates a double touch (double tap or double click) in order to stop the video. Next time we touch the screen, the video will start from the beginning. Now, run the application (`Python kivyplayer.py`), and see how, as soon as you click on the screen, Kivy starts streaming Dan Gilbert's video, *The Surprising Science of Happiness*, from TED (`http://www.ted.com/`):

AsyncImage – creating a cover for the video

In this section, we will learn how to put up a *cover* that will be displayed when the video is not playing. This image will serve as a decoration when the video hasn't started, and in the case of the TED video, it is usually an image that involves the speaker. Let's start introducing a few changes in the code of video.kv:

```
58. # File name: video.kv
59. ...
60. #:set _default_image
        "http://images.ted.com/images/ted/
        016a827cc0757092a0439ab2a63feca8655b6c29_1600x1200.jpg"
61.
62. <Video>:
63.     cover: _cover
64.     image: _default_image
65.     ...
66.     AsyncImage:
67.         id: _cover
68.         source: root.image
69.         size: root.width,root.height
```

In this code, we created another constant (_default_image) with the **set** directive (line 60), and a related property (image) for the Video class that references the constant (line 64). We also created the cover property (line 63) to reference AsyncImage that we added to the Video class (line 66), and that will serve as the cover for the video.

> The main difference between Image and AsyncImage is that the **AsyncImage** widget allows us to continue using the program while the image is loading, instead of blocking the application until the image is completely downloaded.

This is important, since we download the image from the Internet and it could be a big file. When you run the code, you will notice that a waiting image will appear while the image is loading:

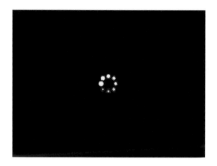

We also set some of the `AsyncImage` properties. We initialized the `source` property (line 68) with the new property (`root.image`) that we created in the `Video` widget to reference the cover image (line 64). Remember that this will internally bind the properties, meaning that each time that we change the `image` property, the `source` property will be updated to the same value. Line 69 repeats the same idea in order to keep the cover's `size` property equal to the dimensions of the video.

 For test purposes, you can replace the URL in `default_image` with the following sample file included with the code: `samples/BigBuckBunny.png`.

We will introduce some changes to our `Video` widget in order to make sure that the cover is removed (hidden) when the video is being played:

```
70. # File name: video.py
71. ...
72. from kivy.properties import ObjectProperty
73. ...
74. class Video(KivyVideo):
75.     image = ObjectProperty(None)
76.
77.     def on_state(self, instance, value):
78.         if self.state == 'play':
79.             self.cover.opacity = 0
```

```
80.        elif self.state == 'stop':
81.            self.seek(0)
82.            self.cover.opacity = 1
83.        return super(self.__class__, self).on_state(instance,
               value)
84.
85.    def on_image(self, instance, value):
86.        self.cover.opacity = 1
87.    ...
```

We changed the **on_state** method to uncover the video when it is playing (line 79), and cover it again when the video is stopped (line 82) using the *opacity* property.

> Avoid removing widgets that are declared in the .kv file. Most of the time, these widgets have internal bounds with other widgets (for example, property bounds), and can cause unexpected runtime errors related to missing internal references and inconsistent bound properties.

Instead of removing widgets, there are several alternatives; for example, firstly, use the **opacity** property to make a widget invisible, secondly, make the widget area equal to zero using the size property (size = (0,0)), and thirdly, use the pos property to place the widget in a location that will never be displayed (pos= (99999,999999)). We chose the first approach; in this case, it is the most elegant. We set the **opacity** property of AsyncImage to make it visible (opacity = 1) or invisible (opacity = 0).

> Even though controlling the cover with the opacity to make it invisible may be the most elegant solution here, you have to be careful because the widget is still there, occupying space on the screen. Depending on the situation, you might have to extend the strategy. For example, if the widget captures some touch events, you can combine the **opacity** and **disabled** properties to hide and disable the widget.

We also created the image property (line 75), and used its on_image associated event (line 85) to make sure that the opacity is restored (line 86) if the image is changed. Now, an image of Dan Gilbert will appear when you run the application (python kivyplayer.py).

Subtitles – tracking the video progression

Let's add subtitles to our application. We will do this in four simple steps:

1. Create a Subtitle widget (subtitle.kv) derived from the Label class that will display the subtitles

2. Place a Subtitle instance (video.kv) on top of the video widget

3. Create a Subtitles class (subtitles.py) that will read and parse a subtitle file

4. Track the Video progression (video.py) to display the corresponding subtitle

The *Step 1* involves the creation of a new widget in the subtitle.kv file:

```
88. # File name: subtitle.kv
89. <Subtitle@Label>:
90.     halign: 'center'
91.     font_size: '20px'
92.     size: self.texture_size[0] + 20, self.texture_size[1] + 20
93.     y: 50
94.     bcolor: .1, .1, .1, 0
95.     canvas.before:
96.         Color:
97.             rgba: self.bcolor
98.         Rectangle:
99.             pos: self.pos
100.            size: self.size
```

There are two interesting elements in this code. The first one is the definition of the size property (line 92). We define it as 20 pixels bigger than the **texture_size** width and height. The **texture_size** property indicates the size of the text determined by the font size and text, and we use it to adjust the Subtitles widget size to its content.

> The **texture_size** is a read-only property because its value is calculated and dependent on other parameters, such as font size and height for text display. This means that we will read from this property but not write on it.

The second element is the creation of the `bcolor` property (line 94) to store a background color, and how the `rgba` color of the rectangle has been bound to it (line 97). The `Label` widget (like many other widgets) doesn't have a background color, and creating a rectangle is the usual way to create such features. We add the `bcolor` property in order to change the color of the rectangle from outside the instance.

 We cannot directly modify parameters of the vertex instructions; however, we can create properties that control parameters inside the vertex instructions.

Let's move on to *Step 2* mentioned earlier. We need to add a `Subtitle` instance to our current `Video` widget in the `video.kv` file:

```
101. # File name: video.kv
102. ...
103. #:set _default_surl
         "http://www.ted.com/talks/subtitles/id/97/lang/en"
104.
105. <Video>:
106.     surl: _default_surl
107.     slabel: _slabel
108.     ...
109.
110.     Subtitle:
111.         id: _slabel
112.         x: (root.width - self.width)/2
```

We added another constant variable called `_default_surl` (line 103), which contains the link to the URL with the corresponding subtitle TED video file. We set this value to the `surl` property (line 106), which we just created to store the subtitles' URL. We added the `slabel` property (line 107), that references the `Subtitle` instance through its ID (line 111). Then we made sure that the subtitle is centered (line 112).

In order to start *Step 3* (parse the subtitle file), we need to take a look at the format of the TED subtitles:

```
113. {
114.     "captions": [{
115.         "duration":1976,
116.         "content": "When you have 21 minutes to speak,",
117.         "startOfParagraph":true,
118.         "startTime":0,
119.     }, ...
```

TED uses a very simple JSON format (https://en.wikipedia.org/wiki/JSON) with a list of captions. Each caption contains four keys but we will only use duration, content, and startTime. We need to parse this file, and luckily Kivy provides a **UrlRequest** class (line 121) that will do most of the work for us. Here is the code for subtitles.py that creates the Subtitles class:

```
120. # File name: subtitles.py
121. from kivy.network.urlrequest import UrlRequest
122.
123. class Subtitles:
124.
125.     def __init__(self, url):
126.         self.subtitles = []
127.         req = UrlRequest(url, self.got_subtitles)
128.
129.     def got_subtitles(self, req, results):
130          self.subtitles = results['captions']
131.
132.     def next(self, secs):
133.         for sub in self.subtitles:
134.             ms = secs*1000 - 12000
135.             st = 'startTime'
136.             d = 'duration'
137.             if ms >= sub[st] and ms <= sub[st] + sub[d]:
138.                 return sub
139.         return None
```

The constructor of the Subtitles class will receive a URL (line 125) as a parameter. Then, it will make the petition to instantiate the **UrlRequest** class (line 127). The first parameter of the class instantiation is the URL of the petition, and the second is the method that is called when the result of the petition is returned (downloaded). Once the request returns the result, the method got_subtitles is called(line 129). The **UrlRequest** extracts the JSON and places it in the second parameter of got_subtitles. All we had to do is put the captions in a class attribute, which we called subtitles (line 130).

The next method (line 132) receives the seconds (secs) as a parameter and will traverse the loaded JSON dictionary in order to search for the corresponding subtitle that belongs to that time. As soon as it finds one, the method returns it. We subtracted 12000 microseconds (line 134, ms = secs*1000 - 12000) because the TED videos have an introduction of approximately 12 seconds before the talk starts.

Everything is ready for *Step 4*, in which we put the pieces together in order to see the subtitles working. Here are the modifications to the header of the `video.py` file:

```
140. # File name: video.py
141. ...
142. from kivy.properties import StringProperty
143. ...
144. from kivy.lang import Builder
145.
146. Builder.load_file('subtitle.kv')
147.
148. class Video(KivyVideo):
149.     image = ObjectProperty(None)
150.     surl = StringProperty(None)
```

We imported `StringProperty` and added the corresponding property (line 142). We will use this property by the end of this chapter when we we can switch TED talks from the GUI. For now, we will just use `_default_surl` defined in `video.kv` (line 150). We also loaded the `subtitle.kv` file (line 146). Now, let's analyze the rest of the changes to the `video.py` file:

```
151.     ...
152.     def on_source(self, instance, value):
153.         self.color = (0,0,0,0)
154.         self.subs = Subtitles(name, self.surl)
155.         self.sub = None
156.
157.     def on_position(self, instance, value):
158.         next = self.subs.next(value)
159.         if next is None:
160.             self.clear_subtitle()
161.         else:
162.             sub = self.sub
163.             st = 'startTime'
164.             if sub is None or sub[st] != next[st]:
165.                 self.display_subtitle(next)
166.
167.     def clear_subtitle(self):
168.         if self.slabel.text != "":
169.             self.sub = None
170.             self.slabel.text = ""
171.             self.slabel.bcolor = (0.1, 0.1, 0.1, 0)
172.
```

```
173.     def display_subtitle(self, sub):
174.         self.sub = sub
175.         self.slabel.text = sub['content']
176.         self.slabel.bcolor = (0.1, 0.1, 0.1, .8)
177. (...)
```

We introduced a few code lines to the on_source method in order to initialize the subtitles attribute with a Subtitles instance (line 154) using the surl property and initialize the sub attribute that contains the currently displayed subtitle (line 155), if any.

Now, let's study how we keep track of the progression to display the corresponding subtitle. When the video plays inside the Video widget, the on_position event is triggered every second. Therefore, we implemented the logic to display the subtitles in the on_position method (lines 157 to 165). Each time the on_position method is called (each second), we ask the Subtitles instance (line 158) for the next subtitle. If nothing is returned, we clear the subtitle with the clear_subtitle method (line 160). If there is already a subtitle in the current second (line 161), then we make sure that there is no subtitle being displayed, or that the returned subtitle is not the one that we already display (line 164). If the conditions are met, we display the subtitle using the display_subtitle method (line 165).

Notice that the clear_subtitle (lines 167 to 171) and display_subtitle (lines 173 to 176) methods use the bcolor property in order to hide the subtitle. This is another trick to make a widget invisible without removing it from its parent. Let's take a look at the current result of our videos and subtitles in the following screenshot:

Control bar – adding buttons to control the video

In this section, we will work on user interaction with the application. Right now, we control the video with touches on the screen that play, pause, and stop the video. However, this is not very intuitive for a new user of our application. So, let's add some buttons to improve the usability of our application.

We will use `Image` widgets enhanced with `ToggleButtonBehaviour` and
`ToggleBehaviour` classes in order to create buttons for a *play/pause* button and
a *stop* button, respectively. Here is a cropped screenshot of the simple *control bar*
that we will be implementing in this section:

Let's start defining our two widgets for `controlbar.kv`. We will cover each widget
one by one. Let's start with the header of the file and the `ControlBar` class definition:

```
178.  # File name: controlbar.kv
179.  <ControlBar@GridLayout>:
180.      rows: 1
181.      size_hint: None, None
182.      pos_hint: {'right': 1}
183.      padding: [10,0,0,0]
184.      play_pause: _play_pause
185.      progress: 0
```

We derived the `ControlBar` class from the `GridLayout` class and set some familiar
properties. We also created a reference to the *play/pause* button, and one new
property (`progress`) that will track the percentage (from 0 to 1) of the progress
of the video. Let's continue with the first embedded widget, `VideoPlayPause`:

```
186.      VideoPlayPause:
187.          id: _play_pause
188.          start: 'atlas://data/images/defaulttheme/
                 media-playback-start'
189.          pause: 'atlas://data/images/defaulttheme/
                 media-playback-pause'
190.          size_hint: [None, None]
191.          width: 44
192.          source: self.start if self.state == 'normal'
                 else self.pause
```

As we will see in `controlbar.py`, `VideoPlayPause` is a combination of `Image` and
`ToggleButtonBehavior`. We implemented the `source` property (line 192) in a way
that changes the image of the widget according to the changes in the `state` property,
`normal` and `down`. Let's now see the code for `VideoStop`:

```
193.      VideoStop:
194.          size_hint: [None, None]
```

```
195.          width: 44
196.          source: 'atlas://data/images/defaulttheme/
                  media-playback-stop'
197.          on_press: self.stop(root.parent.video, _play_pause)
```

Apart from defining some familiar properties, we have bound the event on_press to the stop method (line 197), which will be shown in the corresponding controlbar. py file. Notice that we are assuming that the parent of the root contains a reference to the video (root.parent.video). We will continue working under this assumption in controlbar.py:

```
198. # File name: controlbar.py
199. from kivy.uix.behaviors import ButtonBehavior,
        ToggleButtonBehavior
200. from kivy.uix.image import Image
201. from kivy.lang import Builder
202.
203. Builder.load_file('controlbar.kv')
204.
205. class VideoPlayPause(ToggleButtonBehavior, Image):
206.     pass
207.
208. class VideoStop(ButtonBehavior, Image):
209.
210.     def stop(self, video, play_pause):
211.         play_pause.state = 'normal'
212.         video.state = 'stop'
```

This code imports the necessary classes as well as 'controlbar.kv' (lines 198 to 203). Then, using multiple inheritance, it defines the VideoPlayPause and VideoStop classes as a combination of the Image class and the appropriate behavior (lines 205 and 208). The VideoStop class contains the stop method, which is called when the button is pressed (line 208). This will set the *play/pause* button state to normal and stop the video (line 212).

We will also define a *video controller*, which will be the parent of the *control bar* and *video*, in the videocontroller.kv file:

```
213. # File name: videocontroller.kv
214. <VideoController >:
215.     video: _video
216.     control_bar: _control_bar
217.     play_pause: _control_bar.play_pause
```

```
218.        control_bar_width: self.width
219.        playing: _video.state == 'play'
220.
221.        Video:
222.            id: _video
223.            state: 'pause' if _control_bar.play_pause.state ==
                    'normal' else 'play'
224.
225.        ControlBar:
226.            id: _control_bar
227.            width: root.control_bar_width
228.            progress: _video.position / _video.duration
```

First, we defined five properties for `VideoContoller` (lines 215 to 219): `video`, `control_bar`, `play_pause`, `control_bar_width`, and `playing`. The first three properties reference components of the interface, `control_bar_width` will be used to externally control the width of the *control bar*, and the `playing` property will indicate whether the video is playing or not (line 219).

We then added a `Video` instance (line 221), whose state will depend on the state of the *play/pause* button (line 223), and a `ControlBar` instance. The `width` property of the *control bar* will be controlled by `control_bar_width` (line 227) that we previously created (line 218), and the `progress` property will be expressed as a percentage of the duration (line 228).

Now, we need to create the `VideoController` class in its respective `videocontroller.py` file:

```
229. # File name: videocontroller.py
230. from kivy.uix.floatlayout import FloatLayout
231. from kivy.lang import Builder
232.
233. import video
234. import controlbar
235.
236. Builder.load_file('videocontroller.kv')
237.
238. class VideoController(FloatLayout):
239.     pass
```

We just included the necessary imports, and defined `VideoController` as a derived class of `FloatLayout`. The `kivyplayer.py` file also has to be updated in order to display a `VideoController` instance instead of `Video`:

```
240. # File name: kivyplayer.py
241. from kivy.app import App
242. from videocontroller import VideoController
243.
244. class KivyPlayerApp(App):
245.     def build(self):
246.         return VideoController()
247.
248. if __name__=="__main__":
249.     KivyPlayerApp().run()
```

Feel free to run an application again to test the *play/pause* and *stop* buttons. The next section will introduce a *progression bar* to our application.

Slider – including a progression bar

In this section, we will introduce a new widget called **Slider**. This widget will serve as a *progression bar*, but at the same time it will allow the user to forward and reverse the video. We will integrate the *progression bar* into the *control bar*, as shown in the following cropped screenshot:

As you can see, `Slider` appears to the left of the *play/pause* and *stop* buttons. Let's change `controlbar.kv` to add `Slider` to reflect this order. Let's start with the header of the file and the `ControlBar` class definition:

```
250. # File name: controlbar.kv
251. <ControlBar@GridLayout>:
252.     ...
253.     VideoSlider:
254.         value: root.progress
255.         max: 1
256.     VideoPlayPause:
257.         ...
```

VideoSlider will keep the **value** property updated with the progression of the video. The **value** property indicates the location of the slider on the bar, and the **max** property is the maximum value that it can take. In this case, 1 is appropriate because we express the progression as a percentage (from 0 to 1) of the duration (line 255).

Let's now add the definition of VideoSlider in the controlbar.py file:

```
258. # File name: controlbar.py
259. ...
260. class VideoSlider(Slider):
261.
262.     def on_touch_down(self, touch):
263.         video = self.parent.parent.video
264.         if self.collide_point(*touch.pos):
265.             self.prev_state = video.state
266.             self.prev_touch = touch
267.             video.state = 'pause'
268.         return super(self.__class__,
                 self).on_touch_down(touch)
269.
270.     def on_touch_up(self, touch):
271.         if self.collide_point(*touch.pos) and \
272.             hasattr(self, 'prev_touch') and \
273.             touch is self.prev_touch:
274.             video = self.parent.parent.video
275.             video.seek(self.value)
276.             if prev_state != 'stop':
277.                 video.state = self.prev_state
278.         return super(self.__class__, self).on_touch_up(touch)
```

Controlling the progression of the video with a slider is tricky because the video and the slider need to constantly update each other. The video updates the slider to indicate its progress, and the slider updates the video when the user wants to forward or reverse the video. This creates an entangled logic, in which we have to take into account the following considerations:

1. We need to use touch events because we want to make sure it is the user who is moving the slider and not the video progression.

2. There seems to be an infinite loop; we update the slider, the slider uploads the video, and the video updates the slider.

3. The user might not necessarily just click on the slider, he could potentially drag it, and during the dragging time, the video updates the slider again.

For these reasons, we need to execute the following steps:

1. Pause the video before updating the progression (line 267).

2. Not update the slider directly with the value property, but instead update the video progression with the seek method (line 275).

3. Use the two events on_touch_down (line 262) and on_touch_up (line 270), in order to safely change the progression percentage of the video.

In the on_touch_down method (lines 262 to 268), we have stored the current state of the video (line 265), and a reference to the touch (line 266), and then we have paused the video (line 267). If we don't pause the video, the progression of the video could affect the slider (remember that the value of slider is bound to the progression property in line 254) before we update the video to the progression of the slider. In the on_touch_up event, we made sure that the touch instance corresponds to the one that we stored in the on_touch_down method (lines 272 and 273). Then, we set the video to the right place according to the position of the slider, with the **seek** method (line 275). Finally, we re-established the previous state of the video if it was different from stop (lines 276 and 277).

Feel free to run the application again. You can also experiment with the slider and different options to update the video. Try, for example, a real-time update while you drag the slider through the on_touch_move event.

Animation – hiding a widget

In this section, we will make the *control bar* disappear when the video starts playing in order to watch the video without visual distractions. We need to change the videocontroller.py file in order to animate the ControlBar instance:

```
279. # File name: videocontroller.py
280. from kivy.animation import Animation
281. from kivy.properties import ObjectProperty
282. ...
283. class VideoController(FloatLayout):
284.     playing = ObjectProperty(None)
285.
286.     def on_playing(self, instance, value):
287.         if value:
288.             self.animationVB = Animation(top=0)
289.             self.control_bar.disabled = True
290.             self.animationVB.start(self.control_bar)
291.         else:
```

```
292.                    self.play_pause.state = 'normal'
293.                    self.control_bar.disabled = False
294.                    self.control_bar.y = 0
295.
296.        def on_touch_down(self, touch):
297.            if self.collide_point(*touch.pos):
298.                if hasattr(self, 'animationVB'):
299.                    self.animationVB.cancel(self.control_bar)
300.                self.play_pause.state = 'normal'
301.            return super(self.__class__,
                 self).on_touch_down(touch)
```

Along with the necessary imports at the beginning of the file (lines 280 and 281), we introduced the `playing` property (line 284) and two methods associated with the `on_playing` event and the `on_touch_down` event. The `playing` property was already defined in the Kivy language (line 219), but remember that, due to the file parsing order, we also need to define it in the Python language if we want to use the property in the same class.

When the `playing` property changes, the `on_playing` event is triggered (line 286). This method starts an animation (line 290) and disables the *control bar* when the video is playing (line 289). The animation will hide the *control bar* at the bottom of the screen. The `on_playing` method will also restore the *control bar* (lines 292 to 294), when the video is not playing so it will be visible again.

Since the *control bar* will be hidden when the video is playing, we need an alternate way to stop the video (different from the **Stop** button). This is the reason we included the `on_touch_down` event (line 296). As soon as we touch the screen, the animation, if it exists, is cancelled (line 298), and the *play/pause* button is set to `'normal'` (line 300). This will pause the video and therefore, trigger the `on_playing` event (in this case, because it stopped playing) that we just defined.

You can now run the application again and appreciate how the *control bar* slowly disappears down the bottom of the screen as soon as we press the **Play/Pause** button.

Kivy inspector – debugging interfaces

Sometimes, we encounter problems when we implement our interfaces, and it can be difficult to understand what went wrong, especially when many of the widgets don't have a graphic display. In this section, we will use the application that we created in this chapter to introduce the Kivy **inspector**, a simple tool to debug interfaces. In order to start the inspector, you run the following command: `python kivyplayer.py -m inspector`. You won't notice any difference at the beginning but if you press *Ctrl + E*, a bar will appear at the bottom of the screen, just like the one in the left screenshot of the following image:

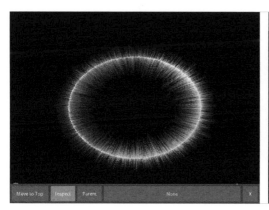 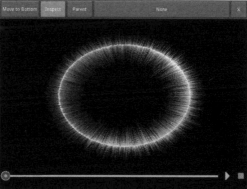

If we press the button **Move to Top** (the first from left to right in the bar), the bar will move to the top of the screen as you can see in the right screenshot, a more convenient position for our particular application. The second button **Inspect** activates or deactivates the inspector behavior. We can now highlight components by clicking on them.

For example, if you click on the *play/pause* button, the video won't play; instead, the button will be highlighted with a red tone as you can see in the following left screenshot:

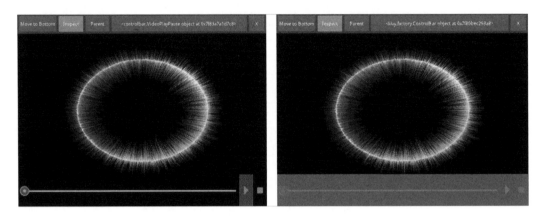

Moreover, if we want to visualize the widget that is currently highlighted, we just have to press the button **Parent** (third left to right on the bar). In the right screenshot, you can see how the *control bar* (parent of the *play/pause* button) is highlighted instead. You should also notice how the long button (fourth left to right on the bar) shows the class that the highlighted instance belongs to. If we click on this button, the entire list of properties for that widget will be displayed, as shown in the following left screenshot:

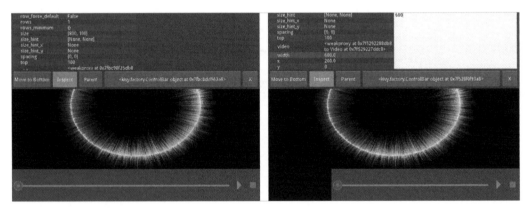

Finally, when we select one of the properties, we are able to modify it. For example, in the right screenshot, we modified the width property of the *control bar*, and we can see how the *control bar* immediately adjusts to the changes.

Remember that since the Kivy widgets are kept as simple as possible, it means that a lot of the times they are invisible because a more complex graphic to display means an unnecessary overload. However, this behavior makes it difficult for us to find errors in the GUI. So when our interface does not display what we expect, the inspector becomes very handy to help us understand the underlying tree structure of the GUI.

ActionBar – a responsive bar

A new set of widgets were introduced in Kivy 1.8.0, all of them related to the **ActionBar** widget. This widget resembles the Android's action bar. This will not only give your applications a modern and professional look, but it also includes more subtle properties such as responsiveness to small screens. Depending on the ActionBar widget hierarchy and components, the different widgets will collapse in order to adapt to the screen space available in the device. First, let's take a look at the final result of our planned ActionBar:

We add the Kivy language code to produce the previous bar in a new file kivyplayer.kv, as presented here:

```
302.  # File name: kivyplayer.kv
303.
304.  <KivyPlayer>:
305.      list_button: _list_button
306.      action_bar: _action_bar
307.      video_controller: _video_controller
308.
309.      VideoController:
310.          id: _video_controller
311.          on_playing: root.hide_bars(*args)
312.
313.      ActionBar:
314.          id: _action_bar
315.          top: root.height
316.          ActionView:
317.              use_separator: True
318.                  ActionListButton:
```

```
319.                    id: _list_button
320.                    root: root
321.                    title: 'KPlayer'
322.               ActionToggleButton:
323.                    text: 'Mute'
324.                    on_state: root.toggle_mute(*args)
325.               ActionGroup:
326.                    text: 'More Options...'
327.                    ActionButton:
328.                        text: 'Open List'
329.                        on_release: root.show_load_list()
330.                    ActionTextInput:
331.                        on_text_validate: root.search(self.text)
```

The hierarchy of the previous code is complicated, so it is also presented in the following diagram:

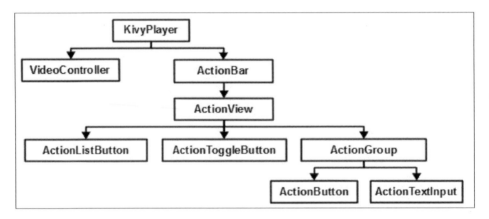

As you can see in the preceding diagram, the **KivyPlayer** contains two main components, the VideoController that we created two sections ago, and the **ActionBar**. If you remember, we created the property playing for the VideoController (line 219), so we bound the associated event on_playing to the method hide_bars (line 311) that later on will basically hide the action bar. Right now, let's focus our attention to the hierarchy of ActionBar.

An **ActionBar** will always contain one **ActionView**. In this case, we just add an ActionView with three widgets: ActionListButton, **ActionToggleButton**, and **ActionGroup**. All of them inherit from **ActionItem**.

An **ActionView** should contain only widgets that inherit from **ActionItem**. We can create our own action items by inheriting from ActionItem.

The **ActionGroup** groups ActionItem instances in order to organize the responsive display. In this case, it contains one **ActionButton** instance and one ActionTextInput instance. ActionListButton and ActionTextInput are personalized widgets that we have to create. ActionListButton will inherit from **ActionPrevious** and ToggleButtonBehaviour, whereas ActionTextInput inherits from **TextInput** and **ActionItem**.

Before continuing, there are a few new properties in the code that deserve an explanation. The **use_separator** property of ActionView (line 317) indicates whether a separator will be used before every ActionGroup. The title property (line 321), which displays a title in the component of ActionListButton, is inherited from ActionPrevious. ActionPrevious is just a button with some extra GUI features (such as the title, but also the Kivy icon that could be modified with **app_icon**), but, more importantly, its parent (ActionView) will keep a reference to it with the **action_previous** property.

Let's now see the definition of ActionTextInput in the actiontextinput.kv file:

```
332. # File name: actiontextinput.kv
333. <ActionTextInput@TextInput+ActionItem>
334.     background_color: 0.2,0.2,0.2,1
335.     foreground_color: 1,1,1,1
336.     cursor_color: 1,1,1,1
337.     hint_text: 'search'
338.     multiline: False
339.     padding: 14
340.     size_hint: None, 1
```

As we said before, ActionTextInput inherits from **TextInput** and **ActionItem**, The **TextInput** widget is a simple widget that displays a text input field in which the user can write. It inherits directly from the Widget class and the **FocusBehaviour** class, which was introduced in Kivy 1.9.0. The multiple inheritance notations that we used (line 333) are new to us.

In order to use multiple inheritance in the Kivy language, we use the notation <DerivedClass@BaseClass1+BaseClass2>.

The **TextInput** widget is one of the most flexible widgets in Kivy and contains a lot of properties that can be used to configure it. We used the background_color, foreground_color, and cursor_color properties (lines 334 to 336) to set the background, foreground, and cursor color, respectively. The hint_text property will display a hint background text, which will disappear when TextInput gains focus (for example, when we click or touch it). The multiline property will indicate whether TextInput will accept multiple lines, and will also activate the on_text_validate event when we hit the *Enter* key, and that we use in the kivyplayer.kv file (line 331).

Notice that we also added a few references in KivyPlayer (lines 305 to 307). We use those references on the Python side of KivyPlayer, which is kivyplayer.py. We will cover this code in three fragments:

```
341. # File name: kivyplayer.py (Fragment 1 of 3)
342. from kivy.app import App
343. from kivy.uix.floatlayout import FloatLayout
344. from kivy.animation import Animation
345. from kivy.uix.behaviors import ToggleButtonBehavior
346. from kivy.uix.actionbar import ActionPrevious
347.
348. from kivy.lang import Builder
349.
350. import videocontroller
351.
352. Builder.load_file('actiontextinput.kv')
353.
354.
355. class ActionListButton(ToggleButtonBehavior, ActionPrevious):
356.     pass
```

In this fragment, we added all the necessary imports of the code. We also loaded the actiontextinput.kv file, and defined the ActionListButton class inherited from ToggleButtonBehaviour and ActionPrevious, as we indicated before.

In fragment 2 of kivyplayer.py, we added all the necessary methods that are called on by ActionItems:

```
357. # File name: kivyplayer.py (Fragment 2 of 3)
358. class KivyPlayer(FloatLayout):
359.
360.     def hide_bars(self, instance, playing):
```

```
361.          if playing:
362.              self.list_button.state = 'normal'
363.              self.animationAB = Animation(y=self.height)
364.              self.action_bar.disabled = True
365.              self.animationAB.start(self.action_bar)
366.          else:
367.              self.action_bar.disabled = False
368.              self.action_bar.top = self.height
369.              if hasattr(self, 'animationAB'):
370.                  self.animationAB.cancel(self.action_bar)
371.
372.      def toggle_mute(self, instance, state):
373.          if state == 'down':
374.              self.video_controller.video.volume = 0
375.          else:
376.              self.video_controller.video.volume = 1
377.
378.      def show_load_list(self):
379.          pass
380.
381.      def search(self, text):
382.          pass
```

For this section, we just implemented the hide_bars and toggle_mute methods. The hide_bars method (lines 360 to 371) hides the *action bar* when the video is playing in a similar way as we hid the *control bar* before. The toggle_button method (lines 372 to 382) uses the **volume** property to toggle between the full volume and mute state. The fragment 3 of the code just contains the final commands to run the code:

```
383. # File name: kivyplayer.py (Fragment 3 of 3)
384. class KivyPlayerApp(App):
385.     def build(self):
386.         return KivyPlayer()
387.
388. if __name__=="__main__":
389.     KivyPlayerApp().run()
```

You can now run the application again. You might want to resize the window to see how the *action bar* reorganizes the components according to the screen size. Here are two examples for medium (left) and small (right) size:

LoadDialog – displaying a directory of files

In this section, we will discuss how to display a directory tree in Kivy in order to select a file. First, we will define the interface in `loaddialog.kv`:

```
390. # File name: loaddialog.kv
391. <LoadDialog>:
392.     BoxLayout:
393.         size: root.size
394.         pos: root.pos
395.         orientation: "vertical"
396.         FileChooserListView:
397.             id: filechooser
398.             path: './'
399.         BoxLayout:
400.             size_hint_y: None
401.             height: 30
402.             Button:
403.                 text: "Cancel"
404.                 on_release: root.cancel()
405.             Button:
406.                 text: "Load"
407.                 on_release: root.load(filechooser.path,
                         filechooser.selection)
```

There is nothing new in this code except for the use of the **FileChooserListView** widget. It will display the directory tree of files. The *path* property (line 398) will indicate the base path of where to start displaying the files. Apart from this, we add the **Cancel** (line 402)and **Load** buttons (line 405), and they call respective functions in the LoadDialog class that is defined in the loaddialog.py file:

```
408. # File name: loaddialog.py
409.
410. from kivy.uix.floatlayout import FloatLayout
411. from kivy.properties import ObjectProperty
412. from kivy.lang import Builder
413.
414. Builder.load_file('loaddialog.kv')
415.
416. class LoadDialog(FloatLayout):
417.     load = ObjectProperty(None)
418.     cancel = ObjectProperty(None)
```

There are actually no explicitly defined parameters in this class definition, just a couple of properties. We will assign methods to these properties in the kivyplayer. py file, and Kivy/Python will call them respectively:

```
419.     def show_load_list(self):
420.         content = LoadDialog(load=self.load_list,
                 cancel=self.dismiss_popup)
421.         self._popup = Popup(title="Load a file list",
                 content=content, size_hint=(1, 1))
422.         self._popup.open()
423.
424.     def load_list(self, path, filename):
425.         pass
426.
427.     def dismiss_popup(self):
428.         self._popup.dismiss()
```

If you remember, the **Open List** button of the ActionBar instance calls the show_load_list method (line 329). This method will create an instance of LoadDialog (line 420), and will send, as parameters of the constructor, two others methods: load_list (line 424) and dismiss_popup (line 427). These methods will be assigned to the load and cancel properties. Once the instance is created, we display it in a Popup (instance line 421 and 422).

Now, the `load_list` method will be called, when we click on the **Load** button of LoadDialog (line 420), and the `dismiss_popup` method when the **Cancel** button is pressed. Don't forget to add the corresponding imports in `kivyplayer.py`:

```
429. from kivy.uix.popup import Popup
430. from loaddialog import LoadDialog
431. from sidebar import ListItem
```

Here is the resulting screenshot, where we can appreciate the tree directory:

ScrollView – displaying a list of videos

In this section, we will display the results of a search performed on the TED video site in a *side bar* that we can scroll up and down, as shown in the following screenshot:

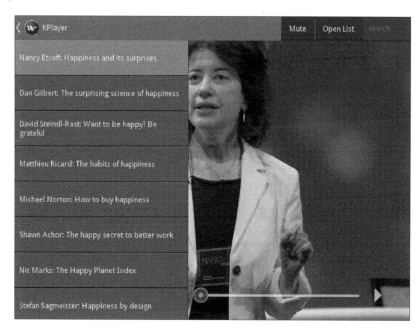

Let's start defining the components of the side bar in the `sidebar.kv` file:

```
432. # File name: sidebar.kv
433. <ListItem>:
434.     size_hint: [1,None]
435.     height: 70
436.     group: 'listitem'
437.     text_size: [self.width-20, None]
438.
439.
440. <Sidebar@ScrollView>:
441.     playlist: _playlist
442.     size_hint: [None, None]
```

```
443.         canvas.before:
444.            Color:
445.                rgba: 0,0,0,.9
446.            Rectangle:
447.                pos: 0,0,
448.                size: self.width,self.height
449.
450.         GridLayout:
451.            id: _playlist
452.            size_hint_y: None
453.            cols: 1
```

The `ListItem` class inherits from `ToggleButton`. The `text_size` property will establish a boundary for the text. If the titles of the videos are too long, two lines will be used instead. The `Sidebar` class inherits from **ScrollView**, which will allow scrolling down the list of videos, similar to the way we scrolled the files in `LoadDialog` of the last section. The `GridLayout` instance inside `Sidebar` is the actual widget that will contain and organize the `ListItem` instances. This is referenced by `Sidebar` in the `playlist` property (line 442)

The contained element inside `ScrollView` has to be allowed to be bigger than `ScrollView` in order to scroll. Set `size_hint_y` to None if you want to add vertical scrolling or `size_hint_x` to None if you want to add horizontal scrolling.

Let's continue with the definition of the sidebar on the Python file (`sidebar.py`):

```
454. # File name: sidebar.py
455.
456. import json
457.
458. from kivy.uix.togglebutton import ToggleButton
459. from kivy.properties import ObjectProperty
460. from kivy.lang import Builder
461.
462. Builder.load_file('sidebar.kv')
463.
464. class ListItem(ToggleButton):
465.     video = ObjectProperty(None)
466.
467.     def __init__(self, video, meta, surl, **kwargs):
```

```
468.            super(self.__class__, self).__init__(**kwargs)
469.            self.video = video
470.            self.meta = meta
471.            self.surl = surl
472.
473.        def on_state(self, instance, value):
474.            if self.state == 'down':
475.                data = json.load(open(self.meta))['talk']
476.                self.video.surl = self.surl
477.                self.video.source =
                       data['media']['internal']['950k']['uri']
478.                self.video.image = data['images'][-
                       1]['image']['url']
```

This file provides the implementation of the ListItem class. There are three parameters in the constructor (line 473): an instance of the video widget, the meta filename that contains metadata of the video as provided by TED videos, and surl that contains the subtitle URL. When the state property of the ListItem widget changes, the on_state method (line 474) is called. This method will open the file provided by TED in a JSON format and extract the necessary information to update the video widget properties. We included in the code of this section, a collection of TED metadata files in the results folder, in order to test the code before you include your own API. For example, results/97.json contains the metadata for the video of Dan Gilbert we have been using so far. You can verify the JSON structure of the lines 477 and 478 in this subtitle file.

Now, we need to add a Sidebar instance to KivyPlayer in the kivyplayer.kv file:

```
479.  # File name: kivyplayer.kv
480.  <KivyPlayer>:
481.      list_button: _list_button
482.      action_bar: _action_bar
483.      video_controller: _video_controller
484.      side_bar: _side_bar
485.      playlist: _side_bar.playlist
486.
487.      VideoController:
488.          id: _video_controller
489.          control_bar_width: root.width - _side_bar.right
490.
491.  (...)
492.
493.      Sidebar:
```

```
494.          id: _side_bar
495.          width: min(_list_button.width,350)
496.          height: root.height - _action_bar.height
497.          top: root.height - _action_bar.height
498.          x: 0 - self.width if _list_button.state ==
                'normal' else 0
```

We have added the `Sidebar` instance and defined some `position` properties based on the other elements of the screen (lines 495 to 498). We also adjusted `width` of the *control bar* to `side_bar` (line 480). When `Sidebar` is displayed, then the *control bar* will adjust automatically to the available space. We control the display of the sidebar with the `ActionListButton` class (line 512), which we are going to define in `kivyplayer.py`:

```
499. # File name: kivyplayer.py
500. import json
501. import os
502.
503. (...)
504.
505. from sidebar import ListItem
506.
507. Builder.load_file('actiontextinput.kv')
508.
509. _surl = 'http://www.ted.com/talks/subtitles/id/%s/lang/en'
510. _meta = 'results/%s.json'
511.
512. class ActionListButton(ToggleButtonBehavior, ActionPrevious):
513.     def on_state(self, instance, value):
514.         if self.state == 'normal':
515.             self.animationSB = Animation(right=0)
516.             self.animationSB.start(self.root.side_bar)
517.         else:
518.             self.root.side_bar.x=0
519.
520. class KivyPlayer(FloatLayout):
521.
522.     def __init__(self, **kwargs):
523.         super(self.__class__, self).__init__(**kwargs)
524.         self.playlist.bind(minimum_height=
                self.playlist.setter('height'))
```

The animation of the sidebar is similar to the others we have seen in this chapter. We also included two global variables: _surl and _meta (lines 509 and 510). These are strings that will serve as templates for the subtitles and metadata files. Notice that %s inside the strings will be replaced. We also introduced a constructor (__init__) to the KivyPlayer class definition (line 522 and 524). Line 524 is necessary to guarantee that the GridLayout instance (inside ScrollView) adapts to its height and therefore, allows scrolling.

We now need to add the ListItem instances to the Sidebar widget. In order to do this, we will define the load_list method (line 525) and the load_from_json method (line 532) in kivyplayer.py:

```
525.     def load_list(self, path, filename):
526.         json_data=open(os.path.join(path, filename[0]))
527.         data = json.load(json_data)
528.         json_data.close()
529.         self.load_from_json(data)
530.         self.dismiss_popup()
531.
532.     def load_from_json(self, data):
533.         self.playlist.clear_widgets()
534.         for val in data['results']:
535.             t = val['talk']
536.             video = self.video_controller.video
537.             meta = _meta % t['id']
538.             surl = _surl % t['id']
539.             item = ListItem(video, meta, surl,
                     text=t['name'])
540.             self.playlist.add_widget(item)
541.         self.list_button.state = 'down'
```

We included a results.json file that contains an example search result list obtained from the TED site. This result is in the JSON format, which you can check in the file. We need to open this file and display its content in the *side bar*. In order to do this, we select the result.json file with the LoadDialog display using the **Open List** button. Once selected, the load_list method is called. The method opens the data and loads the JSON data (line 527). Once loaded, it calls the load_from_json method (line 528). In this method, we create a ListItem instance (line 539) per result obtained from the search on the TED site, and add the instances to the playlist (that is, the GridLayout instance inside the *side bar* (line 451)). The lines 537 and 538 are a common way of concatenating strings in Python. It replaces %s which are present in strings (lines 509 and 510) with the corresponding parameters after %. Now, we will see the results as a side bar list in our application when we open the results.json file as was shown in the screenshot at the beginning of this section.

Search – query the TED Developer API

This final section will introduce a few changes to the code so that we can search the TED site.

 The first thing you need to do is to get an API key from the TED site using the following link:

`http://developer.ted.com/member/register`.

A TED API key is an alphanumeric number (something like `'1a3bc2'`) that allows you to query the TED website directly, and get requests in the JSON format we have been using throughout the last section. Once you receive your API key in your e-mail account, you can modify `kivyplayer.py` and put it in an `_api` global variable. For now, we can use a placeholder like this in the `kivyplayer.py` file:

```
_api = 'YOUR_API_KEY_GOES_HERE'
```

Also, in `kivyplayer.py`, we need to introduce a global variable that contains the search template (`_search`), and replace the content of the `_meta` global variable:

```
_search = 'https://api.ted.com/v1/search.
json?q=%s&categories=talks&api-key=%s'
_meta = 'https://api.ted.com/v1/talks/%s.json?api-key=%s'
```

Notice that the `_meta` variable now has two `%`. Therefore, we will need to replace the `meta = meta % t['id']` code line with `meta = _meta % (t['id'], _api)` inside the `load_from_json` method (line 533). Also, since we are not opening a file, we also need to replace the way we load the JSON in the `ListItem` class since we don't have a file anymore, but a URL. First, we need to import the `URLRequest` class (`from kivy.network.urlrequest import UrlRequest`) at the beginning of the `sidebar.py` file, and then modify the `on_state` method to use the `URLRequest` class as we learned with the subtitles:

```
542.     def on_state(self, instance, value):
543.         if self.state == 'down':
544.             req = UrlRequest(self.meta, self.got_meta)
545.
546.     def got_meta(self, req, results):
547.         data = results['talk']
548.         self.video.surl = self.surl
549.         self.video.source =
                 data['media']['internal']['950k']['uri']
550.         self.video.image = data['images'][-1]['image']['url']
```

We also need to import the `URLRequest` class in `kivyplayer.py`, in order to implement the `search` method in the `KivyPlayer` class definition:

```
551.    def search(self, text):
552.        url = _search % (text, _api)
553.        req = UrlRequest(url, self.got_search)
554.
555.    def got_search(self, req, results):
556.        self.load_from_json(results)
```

Now, you can go and check whether you received your TED API key. Once you have replaced the `_api` variable, you will be able to use the search box in the action bar to query the TED API. You can now use the search on `ActionTextInput`:

 Keep in mind that the API key you just created can identify you and your application as a user of the TED site. All the activity registered with that API is your responsibility. *You shouldn't give this API Key to anyone.*

Controlling the use of your API Key involves setting up your own server, where the API key is safely stored. This server will act as a proxy (`https://en.wikipedia.org/wiki/Proxy_server`) of your application, and it should limit the queries. For example, it should avoid abusive behavior such as a massive number of queries.

Summary

In this chapter, we created an application that integrates many Kivy components. We discussed how to control a video and how to associate different elements of the screen with it. We explored different Kivy widgets and implemented a complex interaction to display a scrollable list of elements. Here is the list of new classes and components that we used in this chapter:

- `Video`: The `allow_stretch` and `source` properties inherited from `Image`; the `state` and `progress` properties; the `_on_load`, `on_eos`, `on_source` and `on_state`, `on_position`, `seek` methods

- `AsyncImage`: The `source` property inherited from `Image`; the `opacity` (inherited from `Widget`) property

- `Label`: The `texture_size` property
- `Slider`: The `value` and `max` properties
- `Touch`: The `double_tap` key
- The Kivy Inspector class
- The `ActionBar`, `ActionView`, `ActionItem` `ActionPrevious`, `ActionToggleButton` `ActionGroup`, and `ActionButton` classes, with `use_separator` of `ActionView` and `title` of `ActionPrevious` properties
- `TextInput`: The `background_color`, `foreground_color`, `cursor_color` and `multiLine` properties
- `FileChooserListView`: The `path` property
- The `ScrollView` class

As a side result of the way this chapter, we have obtained an organized is an enhanced `Video` widget that we can use in other applications. This `Video` widget incorporates synchronization of subtitles that we receive in a JSON format file with the progression of the video and a responsive *control bar*.

We have mastered the use of the `Video` widget. We learned how to control its progression and add subtitles to it. We also covered how to query the TED Developer API in order to get a result lists, and we have practiced our skills manipulating the JSON format. We also learned how to use the Kivy debugger in order to detect errors in our interfaces.

We also made an effort to make our `KivyPlayer` application look professional. We optimized the use of the screen by introducing animations that hide the GUI components when unnecessary. As part of this process, we used many Kivy elements to make our widget consistent, and we reviewed interesting topics such as behaviors, the factory, animations, touch events, and the use of properties in order to create versatile components.

The beginning is at the end, so it is now your turn to start your own applications. I really hope that what you have learned from this book will help you to implement your ideas and start your own application.

Index

G

Gesture class 100
GestureDatabase class 100
gestures
  recognizing 101-106
  recording 99, 100
gestures ToggleButton 106
gesture_to_str string 100
Graphical User Interface (GUI) 3, 55
graphic instructions
  structuring 42-44
GridLayout 17
group property 26
GUI building process 15

H

height property 10
Hello World program 3-6

I

ID 56-58
image list parameter 119
images
  adding 41, 42
Image widget 142
import directive 59
indexes property 39
inheritance
  about 2, 5
  URL 2
instances
  about 2
  URL 2
instruction set
  canvas 42
  canvas.after 42
  canvas.before 42
instruction types
  context instructions 34
  vertex instructions 34

Invaders Revenge game
  Ammo animation, using 120-122
  animations, combining with &
    operator 136, 137
  animations, combining with +
    operator 136, 137
  Atlas, using 118-120
  automatic binding, in Kivy
    language 125, 126
  Boom instance, defining 120
  defining 116, 117
  events, scheduling with clock 128, 129
  fleet, animating 126-128
  Linear transition, defining 122-124
  multi-touch actions, handling 130-133
  shooter, moving with keyboard 134, 135
  sound effects, adding 120

J

JSON format
  URL 151

K

keyboard 135
Kivy
  about 1, 130
  defining 2, 80-83
  properties 80-83
  URL 2
  using 3
Kivy 1.9.0
  URL 86
Kivy API
  URL 15
Kivy Canvas 31
Kivy id 25
Kivy inspector
  about 161
  used, for debugging interfaces 161-163
Kivy language
  events, binding in 74-77
Kivy markup 28
KivyPlayer 164
kivy.uix
  URL 7

Thank you for buying
Kivy – Interactive Applications and Games in Python
Second Edition

About Packt Publishing

Packt, pronounced 'packed', published its first book, *Mastering phpMyAdmin for Effective MySQL Management*, in April 2004, and subsequently continued to specialize in publishing highly focused books on specific technologies and solutions.

Our books and publications share the experiences of your fellow IT professionals in adapting and customizing today's systems, applications, and frameworks. Our solution-based books give you the knowledge and power to customize the software and technologies you're using to get the job done. Packt books are more specific and less general than the IT books you have seen in the past. Our unique business model allows us to bring you more focused information, giving you more of what you need to know, and less of what you don't.

Packt is a modern yet unique publishing company that focuses on producing quality, cutting-edge books for communities of developers, administrators, and newbies alike. For more information, please visit our website at www.packtpub.com.

About Packt Open Source

In 2010, Packt launched two new brands, Packt Open Source and Packt Enterprise, in order to continue its focus on specialization. This book is part of the Packt Open Source brand, home to books published on software built around open source licenses, and offering information to anybody from advanced developers to budding web designers. The Open Source brand also runs Packt's Open Source Royalty Scheme, by which Packt gives a royalty to each open source project about whose software a book is sold.

Writing for Packt

We welcome all inquiries from people who are interested in authoring. Book proposals should be sent to author@packtpub.com. If your book idea is still at an early stage and you would like to discuss it first before writing a formal book proposal, then please contact us; one of our commissioning editors will get in touch with you.

We're not just looking for published authors; if you have strong technical skills but no writing experience, our experienced editors can help you develop a writing career, or simply get some additional reward for your expertise.

Kivy Blueprints

ISBN: 978-1-78398-784-9   Paperback: 282 pages

Build your very own app-store-ready,
multi-touch games and applications with Kivy!

1. Learn how to create simple to complex
    functional apps quickly and easily with
    the Kivy framework.

2. Bend Kivy according to your needs
    by customizing, overriding, and bypassing
    the built-in functions when necessary.

Python Network Programming Cookbook

ISBN: 978-1-84951-346-3   Paperback: 234 pages

Over 70 detailed recipes to develop practical
solutions for a wide range of real-world network
programming tasks

1. Demonstrates how to write various besopke
    client/server networking applications using
    standard and popular third-party
    Python libraries.

2. Learn how to develop client programs for
    networking protocols such as HTTP/HTTPS,
    SMTP, POP3, FTP, CGI, XML-RPC, SOAP
    and REST.

Please check **www.PacktPub.com** for information on our titles

Printed in Great Britain
by Amazon